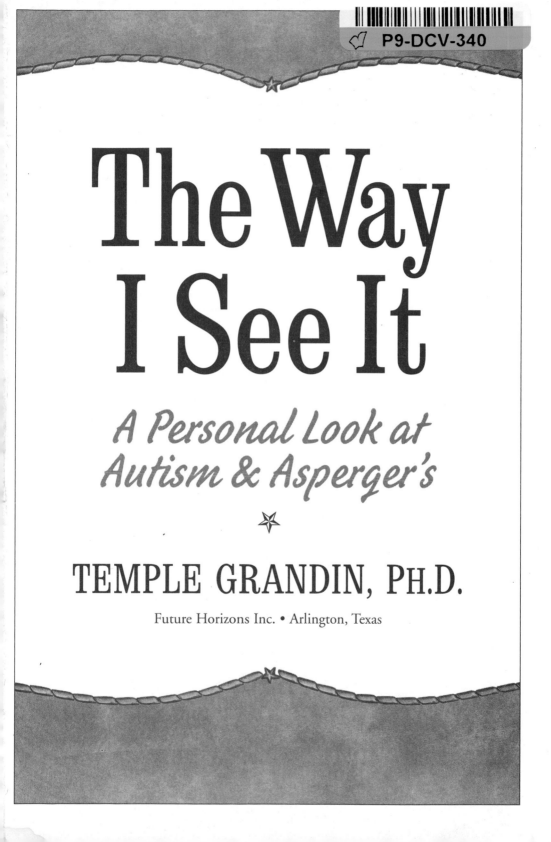

The Way I See It

A Personal Look at Autism & Asperger's

TEMPLE GRANDIN, PH.D.

Future Horizons Inc. • Arlington, Texas

All marketing and publishing rights
guaranteed to and reserved by:

721 W. Abram Street
Arlington, TX 76013
Toll-free: 800-489-0727
Phone: 817-277-0727
Fax: 817-277-2270
Website: *www.FHautism.com*
E-mail: *info@FHautism.com*

Printed in the United States of America

Cover and interior design © TLC Graphics, *www.TLCGraphics.com*
Cover: Monica Thomas; Interior: Erin Stark

ISBN 13: 978-1-932565-72-0

Also by Temple Grandin

*I dedicate this book to all individuals
on the autism spectrum.*

Acknowledgments

I WOULD LIKE TO ACKNOWLEDGE VERONICA ZYSK, MY EDITOR AT Future Horizons, who edited both my articles in the *Autism Asperger's Digest* magazine, and this book. Without her hard work and guidance, this book would not have been possible.

Contents

Contents

Foreword
by Dr. Ruth Sullivan

WHO BETTER THAN TEMPLE GRANDIN TO GIVE US A PERSONAL look at autism and Asperger's?

For over thirty of her nearly sixty years' experience being a person on the autism spectrum, Temple has dedicated much of her time, energy, considerable intellect, and talents to learning about her condition and translating it for the rest of us. This book puts together under one cover her highly insightful, informed, articulate, and most of all, practical, ideas and instructions for dealing with the wide range of behavior, learning styles, and physical health issues found in autism and Asperger's Syndrome.

At the time Temple came on the autism scene, few people had heard of autism, and even fewer had ever heard of someone with autism who could communicate well enough to tell us how it felt, from the inside. I was a member of a small group of parents of children with autism, nationwide, who in November 1965, at the invitation of Dr. Bernard Rimland, met to form a national organization, the National Society for Autistic Children (NSAC), now called the Autism Society of America (ASA). Our goal was to seek a better understanding of this mysterious condition that so severely affected our children, and to seek treatment, as well as cause and cure. There was almost nothing in the literature. Dr. Rimland's book, *Infantile Autism: The Syndrome and Its Implications for a Neural Theory of Behavior* (published in 1964) was among the very first on the subject. None of us knew an adult with autism.

I first met Temple in the mid-1980s at the St. Louis Airport, when making a connection to Chicago for the annual NSAC conference. In the small waiting area there were about 25 other conference goers from across the nation, also waiting for that flight. Most of us knew each other, and the talk was mostly about autism.

Standing on the periphery of the group was a tall young woman who was obviously interested in the discussions. She seemed shy and pleasant, but mostly she just listened. Once in Chicago, she and I got on the conference bus and sat together as we traveled to our hotel. I learned her name was Temple Grandin, and this was her first autism conference. I was impressed at how much she knew about the condition. It wasn't until later in the week that I realized she was someone with autism. I had heard of a woman who had that diagnosis, who was high-functioning, but had not connected the two. I approached her and asked if she'd be willing to speak at the next year's NSAC conference program. She agreed.

Back then, NSAC conferences were the only national meetings focused solely on autism. Each year there was one entire session set aside just for information exchange. It was held in a large room of ten-person round tables, each designated for a special subject, with a discussion leader. That next year I was the discussion leader for a table labeled "Adults with Autism," and that's where Temple first addressed an NSAC audience. The ten chairs were filled immediately, and people were standing at least three deep. The room became noisy, and with so many wanting to hear every word Temple said, I asked for a room just for us. More people followed as we were led to a small auditorium.

Temple and I stood on the slightly elevated stage. The audience couldn't get enough of her. Here, for the first time, was someone who could tell us from her own experience what it was like to be extremely sound sensitive ("like being tied to the rail and the train's coming"). On the topic of wearing certain kinds of underwear, she described her profound skin sensitivity, and how she could not verbally articulate how painful it was. On relationships, she talked about how hard it was to communicate what she felt, and about her difficulty in understanding others. She was asked many questions: "Why does my son do so much spinning?" "What can I do about toilet training?" "Why does he hold his hands to his ears?" "Why doesn't he look at me?" She spoke from her own experience, and her insight was impressive. There were tears in more than one set of eyes that day.

After the hour-long session ended, many stayed around to talk to Temple. She seemed surprised but pleased with the attention—even adulation. Later, when I asked, she said she had been a little nervous. Over the years, I've often thought about that scene, and marveled at how remarkable an event it was for her, and all of us.

Not long afterwards, in 1986, her first book was published, *Emergence: Labeled Autistic*. The rest is history, as they say. Ten years later came her highly acclaimed work, *Thinking in Pictures*, with other autism books to follow. Temple simultaneously became well known for her work and writings in her chosen professional field of animal behavior. She earned a Ph.D. in that discipline, from the University of Colorado. Her 2006 release, *Animals in Translation*, became a *New York Times* Bestseller.

Temple quickly became a much sought-after speaker in the autism community. She wrote articles for the popular press as well as peer-reviewed professional journals. Always generous to projects related to parents and their children, she wrote for parent organization newsletters, and traveled around the U.S. and the world to speak at autism conferences. Probably no one with autism has appeared in the world media more than Temple, nor had a bigger impact on our global understanding of autism and Asperger's Syndrome and the people diagnosed on the spectrum.

Yet, the Temple Grandin of today is not the same woman I met nearly twenty-five years ago. It has been a remarkable privilege to witness Temple's growth in social skills and awareness throughout the time I have known her. She is one of the hardest workers I have ever known. In my opinion, it is mainly that trait that has helped her become the successful, engaging adult she is now, despite severe difficulties along the way. She is knowledgeable. She is willing to help parents as well as others with autism. She is insightful. And she is courageous—a fitting word to explain her heartfelt, strong (and sometimes unwanted) advice to her adult peers with autism or Asperger's on the importance of being polite, dressing appropriately, accepting responsibility for their actions and following rules of civility if they want to get and keep a job or have friends.

And not least, she is funny. Though generally her presentations are straightforward, in recent years she has become quite good at humor. Her audiences love it.

In addition, and to her credit, she has learned to be generous in recognizing those who have helped her along the way, namely her mother, Eustacia Cutler, whose book, *A Thorn in My Pocket*, tells the family story. Others are teachers and colleagues who saw her potential and bravely went beyond current practice to help her develop some of her strengths. For many individuals with autism, it is difficult-to-impossible to understand and develop "theory of mind," that intangible mental process by which most of us intuitively notice and "read" the nuances of social situations: how others are feeling, what they may be thinking, and the meaning behind their nonverbal actions. Temple's persistence in learning this, and her strong analytical skills while doing so, have helped significantly in improving her social thinking and social sense.

Temple continues to wrap her energies around autism and the people it touches. Her talent is a gift to all of us—not just those of us in the autism community, but the world at large. The book you are holding in your hand is the result of her keen detective-like analysis of human beings, her extensive personal thought, and the wisdom gained only through the personal experiences that make up Temple Grandin. It serves as an excellent summary of what one human being has contributed to one of the most disabling and puzzling conditions known to mankind. Temple takes time to listen—without pre-conceived ideas or judgment—to parents and the professionals who work with and for individuals with autism on the entire spectrum, from severe autism to high-level Asperger's. She seeks *solutions*, from teaching strategies to the larger lifespan issues that can present challenges of immense proportions, even for neurotypicals. The suggestions she offers in this book are imaginative, well thought out, practical, and useful. She talks directly to the reader, with honesty and understanding. She knows what autism is like, and her recommendations make sense.

Every library, large or small, needs this book on its shelves. Every school, large or small, with the responsibility of educating children with autism or Asperger's needs the guidance this book offers. Every teacher within those schools will benefit from reading it and applying the strategies Temple so clearly illuminates. Last, and certainly not least, every parent will find within these pages golden nuggets of advice, encouragement, and hope to fuel their day-to-day journey through their child's autism.

As I've heard Temple often remark in the twenty-something years I have known her, about the way she views autism and her life: "I didn't become social overnight. There wasn't a point when some magic switch turned on in my brain and the social stuff made sense after that. I'm the person I am today because of all the experiences I've had, and the opportunities those experiences offered me to learn, little by little. It wasn't easy; sometimes it was really difficult. I've made a lot of mistakes, but I just kept going until I got it right. And, I'm still learning today! That's what I want other people on the spectrum to learn: You just can't give up. You have to keep trying." The wisdom she offers through this book and its personal reflections on autism will, I'm sure, ring true for many more decades to come.

RUTH CHRIST SULLIVAN, PH.D.
May 2008

Ruth Christ Sullivan, Ph.D. was the first elected president of the Autism Society of America (formerly NSAC), founded in 1965 by the late Dr. Bernard Rimland. In 1979 she founded and was Executive Director of Autism Services Center (ASC), in Huntington, WV until her retirement in 2007, at age 83. ASC is a nonprofit, licensed behavioral health care agency that serves all development disabilities but specializes in comprehensive, autism-specific services, in community-based settings including clients' homes. ASC serves approximately 270 clients, with a staff of 350. Dr. Sullivan was one of the chief autism lobbyists for Public Law 94-142 (now known as the Individuals with Disabilities Education Act, IDEA), as well as the Developmental Disabilities Act. She was the main force behind the founding of the West Virginia Autism Training Center at Marshall University, in Huntington, WV, in 1983.

Dr. Sullivan assisted in the production of the 1988 movie, *Rain Man*, serving as a consultant on autism behavior. Dustin Hoffman, who won an Oscar for his starring role as Raymond Babbett, worked directly with Dr. Sullivan and her son, Joseph (born in 1960) who has autism, in practicing for his role. The premiere of *Rain Man* was held in Huntington with Dustin Hoffman and Barry Levinson, the producer, present. It was a benefit event for Autism Services Center.

Though Dr. Sullivan has lived in Huntington, WV for forty years, she is still close to her large, south Louisiana Cajun family in Lake Charles.

For Readers New to Autism

AUTISM IS A DEVELOPMENTAL DISORDER, TYPICALLY DIAGNOSED during the first three years of life. It is neurological in nature, affecting the brain in four major areas of functioning: language/communication, social skills, sensory systems, and behavior. The cause of autism remains a mystery. Current research suggests there may be different subsets arising from genetics, environmental insults, or a combination of both.

Every person with autism is unique, with a different profile of strengths and challenges. No two individuals manifest the same characteristics in the same degree of severity. It is a "spectrum" disorder, and the various individual diagnoses are collectively referred to as autism spectrum disorders (ASD). Individuals on the spectrum range from those who are nonverbal with severe challenges that can include self-injurious behaviors and mental retardation, to individuals on the higher-functioning end of the spectrum (known as Asperger's Syndrome) who are extremely intelligent, with good expressive verbal language, yet markedly impaired social skills and weak perspective-taking abilities.

The rate of autism is now 1 in every 150 births (Centers for Disease Control, 2007) and continues to escalate at alarming rates. Every 21 minutes a child is diagnosed on the spectrum. It is four times more common in boys than girls, and is consistently prevalent around the globe, and within different racial, social and ethnic communities. According to the Autism Society of America, the lifetime cost of caring for one single child with autism ranges from $3.5 - $5 million; the tally for all costs for all individuals approaches a staggering *$90 billion annually.*[1]

Autism is a different way of thinking and learning. People with autism are people first; autism is only one part of who they are. ASD is no longer viewed as strictly a behavioral disorder, but one that affects the whole person on various fronts: biomedical, cognitive, social, and sensory. With individualized and appropriate intervention, children with ASD can become more functional and learn to adapt to the world around them.

Great strides are being made in our understanding of autism and Asperger's and how best to help these individuals. Children are now being diagnosed as early as 12-15 months old, and many who receive intensive early intervention are able to enter elementary school in class with their typical peers, needing minor supports and services. However, no matter the age of diagnosis, children and adults with ASD are constant learners and significant improvements in their functioning can be made at any age with the appropriate types and intensity of services.

(©Autism Asperger's Digest, 2008. Reprinted with permission)

[1] Autism Society of America website, *www.autism-society.org*

Tony & Temple: Face to Face

TEMPLE GRANDIN'S AUTOBIOGRAPHY *EMERGENCE: LABELED AUTISTIC* and her subsequent book, *Thinking in Pictures,* together contain more information and insights into autism than I have read in any textbook. When I first heard one of her presentations, I was immediately aware of her forthright personality. The whole audience was enthralled with her knowledge.

I was delighted to be asked to interview Temple, as it provided an opportunity to seek her counsel on so many topics. She has a remarkably endearing personality and during the interview in San Francisco she entranced an audience of over 300 people. The applause at the end was loud and prolonged.

Temple is my hero. She has my vote for the person who has provided the greatest advance in our understanding of autism this century.

DR. TONY ATTWOOD
World-renowned expert on autism and Asperger's Syndrome

Ed. Note: The following interview was taped live on December 9th, 1999 at a presentation Temple was giving in San Francisco for Future Horizons. The audience loved it! It provided many revealing, and sometimes humorous, glimpses into Temple's life. It was a rare opportunity to see Temple break into hearty laughter. Enjoy!

Tony: Temple, you were diagnosed as autistic when you were fifteen years old. How did your parents present that to you and what did you feel about yourself when you got that information?

Temple: Well, they never really presented it properly. I sort of found out about it in a roundabout way from my aunt. You've got to remember that I'm 53 years old and that was a Freudian era, a totally different time. Actually, I was kind of relieved to find out there was something wrong with me. It explained why I wasn't getting along with the other kids at school and I didn't understand some of the things teenagers did—like when my roommate would swoon over the Beatles. She'd roll around on the floor squealing in front of the Ed Sullivan show. I'd think, yeah, Ringo's cute, but I wouldn't roll around on the floor with him. ...

Tony: So, if you had the job of explaining to a fourteen- or fifteen-year-old that you have autism or Asperger's Syndrome, how would you talk about it today?

Temple: I think I might give them your book and my book. ... Well, I'd probably just explain it in a technical manner: that it's immature development in the brain that interferes with getting along socially. I'm basically a "techie"—that's the kind of person I am. I want to fix things. With most of the things I do, I take the engineering approach; my emotions are simple. I get satisfaction out of doing good work. I get satisfaction when a parent comes to me and says "I read your book and it really helped my kid in school." I get satisfaction from what I do.

Tony: I seem to remember when you were very little and very autistic, there were certain autistic behaviors you really enjoyed doing. What were they?

Temple: One of the things I used to do was dribble sand through my hands and watch the sand, studying each little particle like a scientist looking at it under a microscope. When I did that I could tune the whole world out. You know, I think it's okay for an autistic kid to do a little bit of that, because it's calming. But if they do it all day, they're not going to develop. Lovaas' research showed that kids need forty hours a week connected to the world. I don't agree with forty hours a week of what I call "hard-core applied behavior analysis," just done at a table. But I had forty hours a week of being tuned in. I had an hour and a half a day of Miss Manners meals where I had to behave. Then nanny played structured children's games with me and my sister, ones that involved a lot of turn-taking. I had my speech therapy class every day … these things were very important to my development.

Tony: A moment ago you used the word "calming." One of the problems that some persons with autism and Asperger's have is managing their temper. How do you control your temper?

Temple: When I was a little kid, if I had a temper tantrum at school, mother just said, "You're not going to watch any *Howdy Doody* show tonight." I was in a normal school—twelve kids in a class, a structured classroom. There was a lot of coordination between school and home. I knew I couldn't play mom against the teachers, or vice versa. I just knew if I had a temper tantrum there wouldn't be any TV that night. When I got into high school and kids were teasing me, I got into some rather serious fist fights. I got kicked out of the school for that—it was not good. And then when I went away to the boarding school and I got into some fist fights, they took away horseback riding privileges. Well, I wanted to ride the horses and after I had horseback-riding privileges taken away once, I stopped fighting. It was just that simple.

Tony: But can I ask you, personally, whom were you fighting, and did you win?

Temple: Well … I usually won a lot of the fights …

Tony: So, were you fighting the boys or the girls?

Temple: Both—the people who teased me.

Tony: So you'd actually lay out the boys?

Temple: Oh, I remember one time I punched a boy right in the cafeteria … and then when I stopped fighting, the way I dealt with it was that I would just cry, because it's my way of preventing fighting. I also avoid situations where people are blowing up and getting angry. I just walk away from it.

Tony: I'd like to ask you a technical question. If you had $10 million for research and you were either going to create research in new areas, or support existing research, where would you spend that money?

Temple: One of the areas I would spend it on is really figuring out what causes all the sensory problems. I realize it's not the core deficit in autism, but it's something that makes it extremely difficult for persons with autism to function. Another really bad thing, especially in the high-functioning end of the spectrum, is that as the people get older, they get more and more anxious. Even if they take Prozac or something else, they're so anxious, they have a hard time functioning. I wish there was some way to control that without drugging them totally to death. Then you get into issues like, should we prevent autism? I get concerned about that because if we totally get rid of the genetics that cause autism, then we'd be getting rid of a lot of talented and gifted people, like Einstein. I think life is a continuum of normal to abnormal. After all, the really social people are not the people who make computers, who make power plants, who make big hotel buildings like this one. The social people are too busy socializing.

Tony: So, you wouldn't fund getting rid of Asperger's Syndrome. You don't see it as a tragedy?

Temple: Well, it would be nice to get rid of the causation for the severely impaired, if there was a way we could preserve some of the genetics, too. But the problem is that there are a lot of different interacting genes. If you get a little bit of the trait, it's good; you get too much of the trait, it's bad. It seems to be how genetics works. One thing I've learned from working with animals, when breeders overselect for a certain trait, you can get other bad things that come along with it. For example, with chickens, they selected for fast growth and lots of meat, but then they had problems with the skeleton not being strong enough. So they bred a strong skeleton back into the chicken. And they got a big, rude surprise they weren't expecting. They ended up with roosters that the breeding hens were attacking and slashing. When they bred the strong legs back in, it bred out the rooster's normal courtship behavior. Now, who would have predicted this strange problem? That's the way genetics works.

Tony: Temple, one characteristic you have is that you make people laugh. I think sometimes you may not intend it, but you have a great gift of making people laugh. What makes you laugh? What's your sense of humor?

Temple: Well for one thing, my humor is visually based. When I was telling you about the chickens, I was seeing pictures of them. One time I was in our department conference room at the university. They have framed pictures of all the old department heads, in heavy, thick, wooden frames. I looked at that and said, "Oh, framed geezers!" At another faculty meeting I was looking at them, and I wanted to burst out laughing, thinking about the framed geezers. That's visual humor.

Tony: And, you have a story about pigeons?

Temple: Oh yeah, the pigeon stuff. Wayne and I got rolling around on the ground one night about pigeons. The Denver airport has a lot of pigeons and they don't clean up the dead pigeons in the parking lot. I got to thinking about the places I could put the dead pigeons … like a pigeon hood-ornament for all the city of Denver maintenance trucks. Then they have this place they call the pigeon drop zone. In the parking garage there's this one concrete beam where they all nest … well you don't want to park in the pigeon drop zone. Every time I walk back to the parking garage, I'm wondering what big fancy expensive $30,000 SUV just parked in the pigeon drop zone.

Tony: So, that explains why sometimes you may burst into laughter and other people have no idea what's going on. …

Temple: That's right, it's because I'm looking at a picture in my mind of something that's funny … I can just see that pigeon hood-ornament on a bright yellow Denver city truck—it's just very funny.

Tony: About your family: your mother was a very important part of your life. What sort of a person is she? What did she do personally that helped you?

Temple: She kept me out of an institution, first of all. You've got to remember this was fifty years ago; all of the professionals recommended that I be put into an institution. Mother took me to a really good neurologist and the neurologist recommended the speech therapy nursery school. That was just a piece of luck. The nursery school was run by two teachers out of their house. They had six kids and they weren't all autistic. They were just good teachers who knew how to work with kids. They hired the nanny, when I was three, and the nanny had had experience working with autistic kids. I have a feeling the nanny might have been Asperger's herself, because she had an old car seat out of a jeep that she had in her room—it was her favorite chair.

Tony: How else did your mother help you as a person herself?

Temple: Well, she worked with me a lot. She encouraged my interest in art; she did some drawing things with me. She had worked as a journalist, putting together a TV show on mentally disabled persons and then another TV program on emotionally disturbed children. Of course, back then, fifty years ago, different children were all labeled as emotionally disturbed. As a journalist, she had gone out and visited different schools. So when I got into trouble in ninth grade for throwing a book at a girl—I got kicked out of the school and we had to find another school—she found a boarding school that was one of the schools she had visited as a journalist. If she hadn't done that for me, I don't know what would have happened. Once I got into the boarding school, that's when I found people like my science teacher and my

Aunt Ann, out on the ranch, who were other important mentors. But there were a lot of people along the way who helped me.

Tony: What about your father? Describe your father and grandfather.

Temple: My grandfather on my mother's side invented the automatic pilot for airplanes. He was very shy and quiet; he wasn't very social. On my father's side of the family we have temper problems. My father didn't think I would amount to very much. He wasn't very social either.

Tony: How do you relax? What do you do to calm down at the end of the day?

Temple: Before I took medication I used to watch *Star Trek*—I was very much a Trekkie. One of the things I liked, especially about the old classic *Star Trek*, was that it always had good moral principles. I'm very concerned today about all the violent stuff. It isn't so much how many guns are going off in the movies, it's that the hero doesn't have good values. When I was a little kid, Superman and the Lone Ranger never did anything that was wrong. Today, we have heroes that do things like throw the woman into the water or the woman ends up getting shot; the hero is supposed to be protecting the woman, not letting her get shot. You don't have clear-cut values. And this worries me, because my morals are determined by logic. What would my logic and morals have become if I hadn't been watching those programs, with clear-cut moral principles?

Tony: As we turn to the next millennium, in another 100 years time, how do you think our understanding of autism will change?

Temple: Oh, I don't know ... we'll probably have total genetic engineering and they'll have a Windows 3000 "Make a Person" program. They'll know how to read DNA code by then. We don't know how to do that right now. Scientists can manipulate DNA—take it out and put it in—but they cannot read the four-base source code. One hundred years from now they'll be able to do that. And, I don't think there will be autism, at least not the severe forms of it, because we'll be able to totally manipulate the DNA by then.

Tony: There are a number of persons we've learned about now with autism or Asperger's Syndrome who have written their autobiographies. Who are your heroes in the autism/Asperger's field who have the condition themselves?

Temple: I really look to the people who have made a success of themselves. There's a lady named Sara Miller; she programs industrial computers for factory automation. There's a lady here tonight, very beautifully dressed, who has her own jewelry business, and she told me she has Asperger's. Somebody like that is my hero ... somebody who's making a success of himself or herself, who is getting out there and doing things.

Tony: How about famous people historically, who would you think had autism or Asperger's Syndrome?

Temple: I think Einstein had a lot of autistic traits. He didn't talk until age three—I have a whole chapter about Einstein in my last book. I think Thomas Jefferson had some Asperger's traits. Bill Gates has tremendous memory. I remember reading in an article that he memorized the whole Torah as a child. It's a continuum—there's just no black and white dividing line between a computer techie and say, an Asperger's person. They just all blend right together. So if we get rid of the genetics that cause autism, there might be a horrible price to pay. Years ago, a scientist in Massachusetts said if you got rid of all the genes that caused disorders, you'd have only dried up bureaucrats left!

To conclude, Tony opened up the interview to questions from the audience. Here's one of the best.

Audience member: How did you realize you had control over your life?

Temple: I was not a good student in high school; I did a lot of fooling around. Being a visual thinker, I had to use door symbolism—an actual physical door that I would practice walking through—to symbolize that I was going on to the next step in my life. When you think visually, and you don't have very much stuff on the [mental] hard drive from previous experiences, you've got to have something to use as a visual map. My science teacher got me motivated with different science projects and I realized if I wanted to go to college and become a scientist, I'd have to study. Well, one day I made myself walk through this one door and I said, "Okay, I'm going to try to study during French class." But there was a point where I realized that I had to do some things about my own behavior. And I had experienced some times that were not all that easy, like when my boss got all over me for being a total slob. There were mentors who forced me—and it wasn't always pleasant—but they forced me to realize that I had to change my behavior. People on the spectrum just can't be sitting around complaining about things. They have to actively try to change things. Good mentors can help you do that.

✳

A clinical psychologist from Brisbane, Australia, Dr. Tony Attwood has over thirty years of experience with individuals with autism, Asperger's Syndrome, and Pervasive Developmental Disorder (PDD). He has worked with several thousand individuals, from infants to octogenarians, from profoundly disabled persons to university professors. His books and videos on Asperger's Syndrome and high-functioning autism are recognized as the best offerings in the field. Over 300,000 of his book *Asperger's Syndrome: A Guide for Parents and Professionals* have been sold, and it has been translated into twenty languages.

Introduction

THIS BOOK IS A COMPILATION OF ARTICLES I HAVE WRITTEN FOR THE *Autism Asperger's Digest* magazine over the last eight years. The articles have been grouped into different categories, addressing subjects from early educational interventions, to sensory sensitivity problems, to brain research and careers. At the beginning of each section I have added a new, updated introduction, which includes additional thoughts on the subject matter.

The articles combine both my personal experiences with autism and practical information that parents, teachers, and individuals on the autism spectrum can put to immediate use. The autism spectrum is very broad, ranging from individuals who remain nonverbal to a mild Asperger's individual who is a brilliant scientist or computer engineer. This book contains information that can be applied across the entire autism/Asperger's spectrum.

Diagnosis and Early Intervention

Chapter 1

Do Not Get Hung Up on Labels

Economical Quality Programs for Young Children with ASD

Different Types of Thinking in Autism

Higher Expectations Yield Results

The best thing a parent of a
newly diagnosed child can
do is to watch their child,
without preconceived
notions and judgments,
and learn how the child functions,
acts, and reacts to his or her world.

✦

BOTH RESEARCH AND PRACTICAL EXPERIENCE SHOWS THAT AN intensive early education program where a young child receives a minimum of twenty hours a week of instruction from a skilled teacher greatly improved prognosis. The brain of the young child is still growing and evolving. At this age, the neuropathways are highly malleable, and intensive instruction can reprogram "faulty wiring" that prevents the child from learning. Plus, behaviors in a young child have not yet become ingrained. It will take less practice to change an inappropriate behavior at age 2-3 than it will to change that same behavior at age 7-8. By then, the child has had many years of doing things his way, and change comes about more slowly.

ABA (Applied Behavioral Analysis) programs using discrete trial training have the best scientific documentation backing up their use, but other programs are also effective. The autism spectrum is vast and diversified. Children have different ways of thinking and processing information, and it is important that an intervention method be aligned with the child's learning profile and personality. Detailed descriptions of different types of early intervention programs can be found in a book I recommend: *Early Intervention & Autism: Real-life Questions, Real-life Answers* by Dr. James Ball (2008, Future Horizons, Inc.). While this book is written for parents of newly diagnosed children, more than three-quarters of the information on interventions, effective teaching strategies, program planning, and behavior management is valuable for parents of children of all ages.

My Early Intervention Program

I had a wonderful, effective early education program that started at age two and a half. By then, I had all the classic symptoms of autism: no speech, no eye contact, tantrums, and constant repetitive behavior. In

1949, the doctors knew nothing about autism, but my mother would not accept that nothing could be done to help me. She was determined and knew that letting me continue to exist as I was, was the worst thing she could do. On her own, she found good teachers to work with me—professionals who back then were just as good as the autism specialists today. A talented speech therapist worked with me for three hours a week doing ABA-type training (breaking skills down into small components, teaching each component separately, using repetitive drills that gave me lots of practice) and she carefully enunciated hard consonant sounds so I could hear them. At the speech therapy school, I also attended a highly structured nursery school class with five or six other children who were not autistic. Several of the children had Down Syndrome. These classes lasted about eight hours a week. My nanny was another critical part of my early therapy. She spent twenty hours a week keeping me engaged, for instance, playing repeated turn-taking games with my sister and me. She was instrumental in introducing early social skills lessons, even though at that time it wasn't referred to in a formal manner like that. Within the realm of play, she kept me engaged and set up activities so that most involved turn-taking and lessons about being with others. In the winter, we went outdoors to play in the snow. She brought one sled, and my sister and I had to take turns sledding down the hill. In the summer, we took turns on the swing. We also were taught to sit at the table and have good table manners. Teaching and learning opportunities were woven into everyday life. When I turned five, we played lots of board games such as Parcheesi and Chinese checkers. My interest in art and making things was actively encouraged and I did many art projects. For most of the day I was forced to keep my brain tuned into the world. However, my mother realized that my behaviors served a purpose and that changing those behaviors didn't happen overnight, but gradually. I was given one hour after lunch where I could revert back to autistic behaviors without consequence. During this hour I had to stay in my room, and I sometimes spent the entire time spinning a decorative brass plate that covered a bolt that held my bed frame together. I would spin it at different speeds and was fascinated at how different speeds affected the number of times the brass plate spun.

The best thing a parent of a newly diagnosed child can do is to watch their child, without preconceived notions and judgments, and learn how the child functions, acts, and reacts to his or her world. That information will be invaluable in finding an intervention method that will be a good match to the child's learning style and needs. The worst thing parents can do with a child between the ages of 2-5 is *nothing*. It doesn't matter if the child is formally diagnosed with autism, PDD-NOS or has been labeled something less defined, like global developmental delay. It doesn't matter if the child is not yet diagnosed, but something is obviously "wrong"—speech is severely delayed, the child's behaviors are odd and repetitive, the child doesn't engage with people or his environment. The child must not be allowed to sit around stimming all day or conversely, tuned out from the world around him. Parents, hear this: **Doing nothing is the worst thing you can do.** If you have a three-year-old with no speech who is showing signs of autistic behavior, you need to start working with your child NOW. If signs are appearing in a child younger than three, even better. Do not wait six more months or a year, even if your pediatrician is suggesting you take the "wait and see" approach, or is plying you with advice such as "Boys develop later than girls," or "Not all children start to speak at the same time." My advice to act now is doubly emphasized if your child's language started developing on time and his language and/or behavior is *regressing*.

Parents can find themselves on long waiting lists for both diagnosis and early intervention services. In some cases, the child will age out of the state's early intervention system (birth to three) before his name gets to the top of the list! There is much parents can do to begin working with the child before formal professional intervention begins. Play turn-taking games and encourage eye contact. Grandmothers who have lots of experience with children can be very effective. *Engagement* with the child at this point in time is just as effective as is instruction. While you may not be (yet) knowledgeable about various autism intervention models, you *are* smart enough and motivated enough to engage your child for 20+ hours a week. **Don't wait; act now.**

ADDITIONAL READING

Ball, J. 2008. *Early intervention & autism: Real-life questions, real-life answers.* Arlington, TX: Future Horizons, Inc.

Grandin, T. 1996. *Emergence: Labeled autistic.* New York: Warner Books.

Koegel, L., and C. Lazebnik. 2004. *Overcoming autism: Finding strategies and hope that can transform a child's life.* New York: Penguin Group.

Do Not Get
Hung Up On Labels

D IAGNOSES FOR DISEASES SUCH AS TUBERCULOSIS OR CANCER ARE
precise. Lab tests can tell you the exact types of disease you have.
Unfortunately, a diagnosis for autism, Asperger's Syndrome or PDD-
NOS (pervasive developmental disorder, not otherwise specified) lacks
the precision of medical tests for cancer. There are no lab tests or brain
scans that can be used to definitively diagnose autism spectrum disorders. In the future, precise tests may become available but none exist
today, in 2008.

A diagnosis of a developmental disorder is based on a *behavioral*
profile described in the "doctor's manual" most physicians use: the
DSM-IV (Diagnostic Manual of Mental Disorders, 4th edition), published by the American Psychiatric Association. In making a diagnosis,
doctors consult the manual to see what diagnosis best fits the behavioral profile of the child. Diagnosis of developmental disorders is a
subjective process, and the DSM-IV is just one tool, among many, that
a doctor should rely upon. Many conditions have overlapping symptoms, and the experience of the physician can have a huge impact on
the accuracy of the diagnosis. For instance, a doctor who specializes in
autism spectrum disorders, one who sees a vast range of individuals of
different ages and at different stages of development would be far more
qualified to diagnosis a child on the spectrum than a general pediatrician in a rural area whose familiarity with ASD extends to less than a

handful of individuals. There is often disagreement between psychologists and medical doctors on diagnosis, and some clinicians deviate from the guidelines in the DSM-IV based on their experiences. Some doctors even refrain from making an autism diagnosis because of the emotional impact they fear it will have on the parents.

For a child to be correctly diagnosed with *autism* the child must have delayed or no speech coupled with other impairments in the areas of behavior, social skills, and play skills. Among the behaviors that indicate autism are lack of eye contact, repetitive behaviors such as flapping or rocking, and avoidance or little interest in social interaction. These symptoms must occur before age three and be obvious enough that the child's functioning is markedly different than his typical peers'. Children who fit the diagnostic criteria for *PDD-NOS* have the same early onset of symptoms, but they often display fewer autistic behaviors or in more milder forms. *Asperger's Syndrome* is a milder variant on the autism continuum, with the one main difference being these children have no obvious speech delay. These individuals, too, exist on a spectrum of abilities, and can be easily overlooked because of their language skills and often, advanced intelligence, especially in one area. However, their sensory problems and pervasive social impairments are usually marked, to the trained eye. They are often loners, with few friends, the geeks, the nerds, the socially odd individuals who never seem to fit in. While the average age of diagnosis of autism or PDD-NOS is between three and four years old, children are often not diagnosed with Asperger's until they are eight or nine. Many are misdiagnosed with conditions that share many of the same characteristics, such as ADHD, learning disabilities, or dyslexia. I also want to emphasize that as therapy helps a child improve, a diagnosis is sometimes changed, and in some cases, children can make such progress that they lose their label. However, autism or Asperger's Syndrome is a lifelong condition arising from biomedical, brain-based origins; it never goes away.

There is much controversy about the alarming increase in autism spectrum disorders over the last 10-15 years. Some of this increase is undoubtedly due to broadening the spectrum of autism diagnoses. The addition of Asperger's Syndrome as an "official" diagnosis for education services appeared just in 1994, and since then our awareness of the disorder in both children and adults has skyrocketed as we learn more about this population of individuals. Pediatricians are more aware of autism spectrum disorders now, as are parents, who are more vocal in expressing their concerns with their doctors when something is just not "right" with their child. Despite increased awareness and a broader spectrum of conditions to be diagnosed, I still think there has been a true increase in what is called *regressive autism*. In classic autism, the warning signs are present from birth. With regressive autism, however, a child is developing normally, meeting typical developmental milestones in speech, motor skills and social development, and then loses functioning somewhere at age 18-24 months. Geraldine Dawson, at the University of Washington, has documented the existence of this regressive form of autism by analyzing videos of children's birthday parties. Other autism-savvy researchers who specialize in the early warning signs of ASD, such as Dr. Rebecca Landa at the Kennedy Krieger Institute at Johns Hopkins University in Baltimore, MD, are noticing the same regression. Why this is happening has yet to be determined. Our best guess to date is that these children are born with compromised immune systems then subjected to an environmental insult or combination of insults that opens the door for the autism expression.

The autism spectrum is very broad, ranging from an individual who remains completely nonverbal into adulthood to a brilliant scientist with Asperger's Syndrome who continues to struggle with understanding the social nuances of the world. However the child comes to the diagnosis of autism or PDD-NOS or Asperger's Syndrome, I want to warn parents and teachers: **Do not get hung up on labels.** Labels are useful for obtaining services, to grant a child eligibility into programs or for financial aid services. But the label should never define the child, nor dictate what program should be used with a child. Autism spectrum disorders are varied and no two individuals will manifest the same set of characteristics at the same level of intensity. Always look at the child—not the label—and base treatment decisions on the child's individual profile of strengths and weaknesses, learning style, personality, etc. It would be easier for parents and educators if, like with cancer or diabetes, we could equate the label with a proven form of treatment. Diagnosed with autism? Use treatment programs X, Y, or Z. Diagnosed with Asperger's? Instead use program C, D, or E. That is not the case; it may never be the case. Far too often we adults make gross assumptions about the capabilities of people with ASD based on their label, especially with children who are nonverbal or have limited verbal abilities. **NEVER** let a label lower your reasonable expectations of a child and that child's capacity for learning. By doing so, you rob the child of the very experiences and opportunities that can allow learning to grow and develop. You rob the child of his potential, and his future. All because of a label?

The boundaries that separate the developmental disorders are fuzzy and imprecise. There are no black and white dividing lines between autism, PDD-NOS, and Asperger's Syndrome. It is a very broad spectrum and the more we learn about these individuals, the greater appreciation we have for the myriad strengths and challenges these individuals display. Let us not limit the lives of these children and adults by our own preconceived notions based on the label attached to them. See the person, not the label.

REFERENCE

American Psychiatric Association. 1994. *Diagnostic and statistical manual IV*, Washington, D.C.

Economical Quality Programs for Young Children with ASD

I WAS LUCKY TO GET STATE-OF-THE-ART EARLY INTERVENTION (EI) AND education while growing up in the early 1950s. Despite the lack of knowledge on autism and how to treat it (aside from institutionalization, which was the norm at that time), my mother had me in an excellent speech therapy nursery school by age three and I had a nanny who spent hours and hours per week playing turn-taking games and structured, enjoyable activities with me. In addition, our household's behavior rules were well-defined and social manners and social expectations were strictly enforced. Fortunately, my parents had enough money to pay for the programs that contributed to my development and laid the foundations for successful functioning as I grew up and ventured out on my own. Adjusting the fees for inflation, the cost of my program would probably be in the mid-range, compared to early intervention programs being used today. Many programs now available are much more expensive.

Can parents on a limited budget put together a good program for their young autistic child? The answer is yes, with a little thought and planning. I have talked to parents who have put together their own successful EI program after reading a few books and enlisting the help of volunteers. Self-motivation and an unfailing desire to help their child are needed as much as is education about autism. The absolute worst thing a parent can do is to let their child sit and watch TV all day or zone out unaware of his or her surroundings. This is precious time wasted, never to be regained.

Both research and practical experience has indicated that twenty or more hours of intense one-to-one interaction with an adult improves language and other behaviors in children with ASD. In many parts of the country a public school will provide only one or two hours a week of therapy with a speech therapist, an occupational therapist (OT), or a behavioral specialist. This is not enough to be really effective; therefore, parents need to take the lead and provide supplemental instruction themselves.

I recommend that parents in those situations approach the school therapists as "coaches" who can educate them on their child's autism and teach them how to do more intensive therapy at home. It also helps if family members or volunteers who are working with the child (for instance, a grandmother who has volunteered to work with a four year old) visit the school every week and watch the professional therapist work with the child. Invaluable information can be gleaned by watching sessions "in action" that no amount of reading will ever convey. Conversely, it might also be helpful from time to time to pay the therapist to spend an hour or two observing how the in-home program is unfolding. Sometimes a small change to a program can make a world of difference and it often takes a trained eye to spot situations like this. The weekly get-togethers are also a perfect time to discuss the child's progress and review goals and objectives for the coming week so everyone can keep track of progress and program changes.

Church and civic groups are a great place to find people who might be willing to work with a child. Other sources of help include students from the local high school or college students. When looking for volunteers to help teach the child, try to be specific about the types of things they will be doing. For instance, grandmothers might feel comfortable volunteering to "play" with a child, or help provide "simple structured, repetitive drills"—those are familiar skills most people possess. Yet the same grandmother might feel ill-equipped if you ask them to "help out with the therapeutic behavior program designed for a child with autism." Most people don't know what that type of program entails, and they may think that only someone with a college degree would have relevant skills. Be sure to mention that you (or someone else) will be providing them with basic education and training on autism to further reinforce their ability to handle what comes up. Many people are genuinely interested in helping others, provided they get some training on how to do it.

I have observed that some teachers and therapists have a knack for working with children with ASD and others do not. Passive approaches do not work. Parents need to find the people, both professionals and non-professionals, who know how to be gently insistent, who keep the child motivated to learn, are child-centered in their approach, and are dedicated to teaching children with autism in a way they can learn, instead of insisting the child learn in the way they teach. Doing so naturally engages the child, which is the foundation of any effective program for children with autism, no matter what the cost.

Strategies that build on
the child's area of strength
and appeal to their thinking
patterns will be most effective.

Different Types of
Thinking in Autism

RECENT STUDIES ON THE BRAIN, AND ESPECIALLY THE BRAINS OF people diagnosed with autism spectrum disorders, are shedding light on the physiological underpinnings of our thoughts and emotions. We are gaining a better understanding of how neuropathways are formed and the extent to which biology influences behavior.

When I was much younger, I assumed that everybody perceived the world the same way I did, that is, that everybody thought in pictures. Early in my professional career I got into a heated verbal argument with an engineer at a meat-packing plant when I told him he was stupid. He had designed a piece of equipment that had obvious flaws to me. My visual thinking gives me the ability to "test-run" in my head a piece of equipment I've designed, just like a virtual reality computer system. Mistakes can be found prior to construction when I do this. Now I realize his problem was not stupidity; it was a lack of visual thinking. It took me years to learn that the majority of people cannot do this, and that visualization skills in some people are almost nonexistent.

All minds on the autism/Asperger's spectrum are detail-oriented, but how they specialize varies. By questioning many people both on and off the spectrum, I have learned that there are three different types of specialized thinking:

- Visual thinking/Thinking in Pictures, like mine
- Music and Math thinking
- Verbal logic thinking

Since autism is so variable, there may be mixtures of the different types. The importance of understanding these three ways of thinking comes into play when trying to teach children with ASD. Strategies that build on the child's area of strength and appeal to their thinking patterns will be most effective. This is most likely to become evident between the ages of five and eight. In children younger than five, it is often difficult to identify their strengths yet, unless savant skills are unfolding.

Visual Thinkers

These children often love art and building blocks, such as Legos. They get easily immersed in projects. Math concepts such as adding and subtracting need to be taught starting with concrete objects the child can touch. Drawing and other art skills should be encouraged. If a child only draws one thing, such as airplanes, encourage him to draw other related objects, such as the airport runways, or the hangars, or cars going to the airport. Broadening a child's emerging skills helps him be more flexible in his thinking patterns. Keep in mind that verbal responses can take longer to form, as each request has to be translated from words to pictures before it can be processed, and then the response needs to be translated from pictures into words before it is spoken.

Music and Math Thinkers

Patterns instead of pictures dominate the thinking processes of these children. Both music and math are a world of patterns, and children who think this way can have strong associative abilities. They like finding relationships between numbers or musical notes; some children may have savant-type calculation skills or be able to play a piece of music after hearing it just once. Musical talent often emerges without formal instruction. Many of these children can teach themselves if key-boards and other instruments are available.

Verbal Logic Thinkers

These children love lists and numbers. Often they will memorize bus timetables and events in history. Interest areas often include history, geography, weather, and sports statistics. Parents and teachers can use these interests and talents as motivation for learning less-interesting parts of academics. Some verbal logic thinkers are whizzes at learning many different foreign languages.

The thinking patterns of individuals with ASD are markedly different from the way in which "normal" people think. Because of this, too much emphasis is placed on what they "can't do." While impairments and challenges do exist, greater progress can be made teaching these individuals when parents and teachers work on building the child's strengths and teach in a manner that is aligned with their basic pattern of thinking.

My life and career could have been
derailed and wrecked if my mother
and business associates
had not pushed me to do things.

✮

Higher Expectations
Yield Results

YOUNG CHILDREN WITH AUTISM SPECTRUM DISORDERS DO NOT learn by listening to and watching others, as do typical children. They need to be specifically taught things that others seem to learn by osmosis. A good teacher is gently insistent with a young autistic child in order to get progress. The teacher has to be careful not to cause sensory overload, but at the same time has to be somewhat intrusive into the child's world of stimming or silent withdrawal in order for the child to engage in learning.

When children get a little older, they need to be exposed to many different things to stimulate their continued learning in different areas of life. There also need to be expectations for proper social behavior. When I look back at my life, my mother made me do a number of things I did not like, but these activities were really beneficial. They gave me opportunities to practice social skills, converse with less-familiar people, develop self-esteem and learn to negotiate unanticipated changes. None of these activities caused major problems with sensory oversensitivity. While Mother may have pushed me to do things, she understood well that a child should never be forced into a situation that includes painful sensory stimulation.

By age five, I was required to dress up and behave in church and sit through formal dinners both at home and at Granny's. When I didn't, there was a consequence, and I lost a privilege that meant something to me. Fortunately, our church had a beautiful old-fashioned organ I liked. Most of the service was boring to me, but that organ made it somewhat tolerable to sit through. A modern church with loud, amplified music probably would be sensory overload to someone like me.

When I was reluctant to learn to ride a bike, I was urged to learn. Mother was always testing the limits on how far she could push me. I became motivated to learn after I missed a bike trip to the Coca-Cola plant.

When I was a teenager, the opportunity arose for me to visit my aunt's ranch in Arizona. At the time, I was having non-stop panic attacks and was afraid to go. Mother made me go anyway, telling me I could come home in two weeks. When I got there, I loved it and stayed all summer. Aunt Ann became one of my important mentors. My career in livestock equipment design would have never started if I had been allowed to stay home.

I often needed a certain amount of pushing to do new things by myself. I was good at building things, but afraid to go to the lumber yard and buy the wood by myself. Mother made me do it. She never let my autism be an excuse for not trying something she knew would be beneficial for me to learn. I came back crying from that outing, but I had the wood with me. Further trips to the lumber yard were easy. At one of my early jobs my boss made me "cold call" cattle magazines to get articles published. After I got over the initial fear, I found I was good at getting articles into national cattle publications. In all of the above cases, either my mother or a boss had to push me to do things even though I was afraid. Yet the things I learned—especially about myself—were priceless.

After I started my freelance design business, I almost gave it up because an early client was not 100% satisfied. My black-and-white thinking led me to believe that clients would always be 100% satisfied. Fortunately, my good friend Jim Uhl, the contractor who built my systems, would not let me quit. He actively kept pushing and talking to me and asking for the next drawing. When I produced a new drawing, he praised it. Now I know that 100% client satisfaction is impossible.

My life and career could have been derailed and wrecked if my mother and business associates had not *pushed* me to do things. Mother did not let me lie around the house, and never viewed my autism as rendering me incapable. Business associates stayed after me and made me do things. These adult mentors are a grown-up version of a good special education teacher who is gently insistent with a three-year-old child with autism. What it demonstrates overall is that people with ASD can learn and succeed when others around them believe in their abilities and hold high expectations of them.

Teaching and Education

Chapter 2

Good teachers understand
that for a child to learn,
the teaching style
must match the student's
learning style.

✹

E VERY CHILD WITH ASD HAS HIS OR HER OWN PERSONALITY AND profile of strengths and weaknesses; this is no different than with typical children. They can be introverts or extroverts, have a sunny disposition or be cranky, love music or math. Parents and educators can easily forget this, and attribute every action or reaction of the child to autism or Asperger's, and therefore in need of dissection and "fixing." The way I see it, the goal in teaching children with autism is not to turn them into clones of their typical peers (i.e., "normal"). When you think about it, not all characteristics exhibited by typical people are worthy of being modeled. A much more meaningful perspective is to teach this population the academic and interpersonal skills they need to be *functional* in the world and use their talents to the best of their ability. Autism is not a death sentence for a child or the family. It brings with it great challenges, but it can also bring to the child the seeds of great talents and unique abilities. It is the responsibility of parents and educators to find those seeds, nurture them, and make sure they grow. That should be the goal of teaching and education for children with ASD too, not just for typical children.

The different thinking patterns of individuals with ASD require parents and educators to teach from a new frame of reference, one aligned with their autism way of thinking. Expecting children with ASD to learn via the conventional curriculum and teaching methods that "have always worked" for typical children is to set everyone up for failure right from the start. It would be like placing a young child on a grown up's chair and expecting his feet to reach the floor. That's just silly, isn't it? Yet, surprisingly, that is still how many schools and educators approach students with ASD. Good teachers understand that for a child to learn, the teaching style must match the student's learning style. With autism and especially with Asperger's students, it is not enough to match the teaching style to the child's learning style. Educators must take this idea one step further, and be continuously mindful that students with ASD come to school without a developed social thinking framework. This is the aspect of ASD that can be difficult for adults to understand, envision, and work around. Our public education system is built upon the premise that children enter school with basic social functioning skills in place. Kids with autism—with their characteristic social thinking challenges—enter school already lagging far behind their classmates. Teachers who don't recognize this, and make accommodations to teach social thinking and social skills alongside traditional academics, just further limit the opportunities children with ASD have to learn and grow.

To Mainstream or Not to Mainstream?

At age five I started attending a small school with typical children. In today's language, that would be called mainstreaming. It is important to note that this worked for me because the structure and composition of the class was well matched to my needs. The school had highly structured old-fashioned classes with only twelve students. Children were expected to behave and there were strict rules, enforced consistently, and with consequences applied for infractions. The environment was relatively quiet and controlled, without a high degree of sensory stimulation. In this environment I did not need an aide. Contrast that classroom with today's learning environment. In a class of thirty students, with a single teacher, in a less structured classroom within a larger school, I would never have survived without the direct assistance of a one-on-one aide.

Whether or not to mainstream an elementary school child on the autism spectrum is a decision that should take many factors into consideration. After countless discussions with parents and teachers, I have come to the conclusion that much depends on the particular school and the particular teachers in that school. The idea of mainstreaming is a worthy goal, and in an ideal situation—where all the variables are working in favor of the child with ASD—it can be a highly positive experience. But the reality of the situation is often the opposite: lack of teacher training, large classes, limited opportunities for individual modifications, and lack of funding to support one-on-one paraprofessionals can render this environment disastrous for the spectrum child. For elementary school children on the higher functioning end of the autism spectrum, I usually favor mainstreaming because it is essential for them to learn social skills from typically developing children. If a child is homeschooled or goes to a special school, it is imperative that the child has regular engagement with typical peers. For nonverbal children, mainstreaming works well in some situations—again, much depends on the school, its expertise in autism, and its program. A special school may be a better choice for the nonverbal or cognitively impaired child with autism, especially in cases where severe, disruptive behavior problems exist and need to be addressed.

Parents frequently ask me whether or not they should change the school or program their child is in. My response is to ask this question: "Is your child making progress and improving where he is now?" If they say he is, I usually recommend staying in the school or the program and then discuss whether some additional services or program modifications may be needed. For instance, the child may do even better with more attention to physical exercise, or addressing his sensory problems, or adding a few more hours of individualized ABA (Applied Behavior Analysis) therapy or social skills training. However, if the child is making little or no progress, and the school's attitude is not supportive or accommodating of the different needs and learning styles of children with ASD so the parent is constantly battling for even the most basic services, it may be best to find a different school or program. This will, of course, require time and effort on the part of the parent, but it is important for parents to keep the end goal in sight—giving the child as much opportunity to learn and acquire needed skills in as supportive an environment as possible. It does no one good, and least of all the child, for a parent to repeatedly fight a school system, either within IEP meetings or through due process, to win their case within an environment of individuals who are not interested in truly helping the child. Sadly, this scenario plays out in schools and districts across the country. Valuable time that could be spent in meaningful instruction that helps the child is wasted while the school and parent butt heads for not just months, but in many cases, *years*. The child—and the child's needs—should always remain the focus. If the school is not child-focused, then parents should find one that is.

I reiterate a point made earlier: so much depends on the *particular people* working with the child. In one case, a third grader in a good school with an excellent reputation had several teachers who simply did not like him, nor did they attempt to understand his learning style and modify instruction to meet that style. The child hated going to school. I suggested the parents try to find a different school. They did, and the child is now doing great in his new school. In my conversations with parents and teachers, I have also observed that it doesn't matter whether the elementary school is public or private; this is seldom the issue. More depends on local conditions: the school's perception of children with disabilities and philosophy towards their education, the extent to which staff have been trained/receive ongoing training on autism spectrum disorders and how best to work with this population, and the support provided by administration to staff in educating these students. Decisions must be made on a case-by-case basis.

The Parent Guilt Trip

It is unfortunate, but a reality of today's society, that some individuals and companies who run special schools, sell therapy services, or market products to the autism community often try to put parents on a guilt trip. All parents want what's best for their child, and parents of newly diagnosed children can be especially vulnerable. These vendors prey upon parents' emotions in advertising and personal encounters, suggesting that parents are not good parents if they don't try their program or product, or that by not using whatever it is they offer, the parent isn't doing "everything possible" to help their child. Some go as far as to tell parents that their child is doomed unless they use their program or product. One parent called me about a situation just like this. The family was ready to sell their house to have the funds needed to send their four-year-old child with autism to a special school in another state. I asked him if the child was learning and making progress at the local public school. The dad told me he was. Yet, the special school was making great claims about the progress their child would make with them. I talked with the dad about the negative impact disrupting the child's life like this might have, taking him away from his family and familiar surroundings, and sending him to a school in another state. The very real possibility existed that the child could get worse, rather than better. By the time we ended our conversation, the parents decided to keep their child in his local school and supplement his education with some additional hours of one-to-one therapy.

The articles in this section shed light on the different thinking and learning patterns of children with ASD. They offer many teaching tips to help children succeed. Among the different topics covered are areas that I view as especially important: developing the child's strengths, using a child's obsessions to motivate schoolwork, and teaching the child problem-solving and thinking skills that will assist him not just during his limited years in school, but throughout his entire life.

✫

BOOKS THAT GIVE INSIGHT INTO
AUTISTIC THINKING AND LEARNING PATTERNS

Grandin, T. (2005). *Unwritten Rules of Social Relationships: Decoding Social Mysteries Through the Unique Perspectives of Autism.* Arlington, TX: Future Horizons, Inc.

Grandin T. (2006). *Thinking in Pictures* (Expanded Edition). New York: Vintage Press/Random House.

Tammet D. (2007). *Born on a Blue Day: Inside the Extraordinary Mind of an Autistic Savant.* New York: Free Press.

Teachers and parents need
to help both children and adults
with autism take all the little details
they have in their head and put them
into categories to form concepts
and promote generalization.

Autism The Way I See It

Teaching How to Generalize

MANY CHILDREN AND PEOPLE WITH AUTISM ARE NOT ABLE TO TAKE all the facts they know and link them together to form concepts. What has worked for me is to use my visual thinking to form concepts and categories. Explaining how I do this may help parents and professionals teach children with autism how to form concepts and generalizations.

When I was a little child, I knew that cats and dogs were different because dogs were bigger than cats. When the neighbors bought a little Dachshund, I could no longer categorize dogs by size. Rosie the Dachshund was the same size as a cat. I can remember looking intently at Rosie to find some visual characteristic that both our Golden Retriever and Rosie had in common. I noticed that all dogs, regardless of size, had the same kind of nose. Therefore, dogs could be placed in a separate category from cats because there are certain physical features that every dog has that no cat has.

Categorizing things can be taught. Little kindergarten children learn to categories all the red objects or all the square objects. Irene Pepperberg, a scientist at the University of Arizona, has taught her parrot, Alex, to differentiate and identify objects by color and shape. He can pick out all the red square blocks from a tray containing red balls, blue square blocks, and red blocks. He understands categorization of objects by color, shape, and size. Teaching children and adults with autism to categorize and form concepts starts first with teaching simple categories such as color and shape. From this, we can help them understand that certain facts they have memorized can be placed in one category and other facts can be placed in another category.

Teaching Concepts such as Danger

Many parents have asked me, "How do I teach my child not to run into the street?" or "He knows not to run into the street at our house, but at Grandma's he runs into the street." In the first situation, the child actually has no concept of danger at all; in the second, he is not able to generalize what he has learned at home to a new house and street.

Danger as a concept is too abstract for the mind of a person who thinks in pictures. I did not understand that being hit by a car would be dangerous until I saw a squashed squirrel in the road and my nanny told me that it had been run over by a car. Unlike the cartoon characters on TV, the squirrel did not survive. I then understood the cause and effect of being run over.

After the squirrel incident, how did I learn that all cars on all streets are dangerous? It is just like learning concepts like the color red or square versus round. I had to learn that no matter where I was located, all cars and all streets had certain common features. When I was a child, safety concepts were drilled into my head with a book of safety songs. I sang about always looking both ways before crossing a street to make sure a car was not coming. To help me generalize, my nanny took my sister and me for walks around the neighborhood. On many different streets she had me look both ways before crossing. This is the same way that guide dogs for the blind are trained. The dog must be able to recognize stop lights, intersections and streets in a strange place. During training, he is taken to many different streets. He then has visual, auditory and olfactory (smell) memories of many different streets. From these memories, the dog is able to recognize a street in a strange place.

For either the guide dog or the person with autism to understand the concept of *street*, they have to see more than one street. Autistic thinking is specific to general. To learn a concept of *dog* or *street*, I had to see many specific dogs or streets before the general concept could be formed. A general concept such as *street* without pictures of many specific streets stored in my memory bank is absolutely meaningless.

Autistic thinking is always detailed and specific. Teachers and parents need to help both children and adults with autism take all the little details they have in their head and put them into categories to form concepts and promote generalization.

Interests and talents
can turn into careers.

★

The Importance
of Developing Talent

THERE IS OFTEN TOO MUCH EMPHASIS IN THE WORLD OF AUTISM on the deficits of these children and not enough emphasis on developing the special talents that many of them possess. Talents need to be developed because they can form the basis of skills that will make a person with autism or Asperger's employable. Abilities such as drawing or math skills need to be nurtured and expanded. If a child likes to draw trains, that interest should be broadened into other activities, such as reading a book about trains or doing a math problem calculating the time it would take to travel from Boston to Chicago.

It is a mistake to stamp out a child's special interests, however odd they may seem at the time. In my own case, my talent in art was encouraged. My mother bought me professional art materials and a book on perspective drawing when I was in grade school.

Fixations and special interests should be directed into constructive channels instead of being abolished to make a person more "normal." The career I have today as a designer of livestock facilities is based on my talent areas. I use my visual thinking to design equipment. As a teenager, I became fixated on cattle squeeze chutes after I discovered that when I got in a cattle squeeze chute it relieved my anxiety. Fixations can be great motivators if they are properly channeled. My high school teacher directed my interest in cattle chutes into motivating me to study science and to study more in school. He told me that if I learned more about the field of sensory perception, I could find out why the pressure applied by the cattle chute was relaxing. Now, instead of boring everybody I knew with endless talk about cattle chutes, I immersed myself in the study of science. My original interest in the cattle chute also led to an interest in the behavior of cattle, then the design of systems, which led to the development of my career.

This is an example of taking a fixation and broadening it out into something constructive. Sometimes teachers and parents put so much emphasis on making a teenager more social that developing talents is neglected. Teaching social skills is very important, but if the person with autism is stripped of all their special interests, they may lose meaning in their life. "I am what I think and do, more than what I feel." Social interactions can be developed through shared interests. I had friends as a child because other children liked making craft projects with me. During the difficult years of high school, special interest clubs can be a lifesaver.

Recently I watched a TV documentary about autism. One of the people profiled liked to raise chickens. Her life took on meaning when she discovered that other people shared the same hobby. When she joined a poultry hobby club, she received social recognition for being an expert.

Interests and talents can turn into careers. Developing and nurturing these unique abilities can make life more fulfilling for a person with autism.

Teaching People
with Autism/Asperger's
to be More Flexible

RIGIDITY IN BOTH BEHAVIOR AND THINKING IS A MAJOR CHARAC-
teristic of people with autism and Asperger's. They have difficulty
understanding the concept that sometimes it is okay to break a rule. I
heard about a case where an autistic boy had a severe injury but he did
not leave the school bus stop to get help. He had been taught to stay
at the bus stop so that he would not miss the bus; he could not break
that rule. Common sense would have told most people that getting
help for a severe injury would be more important than missing the
bus. But not to this young man.

How can common sense be taught? I think it starts with teaching
flexibility at a young age. Structure is good for children with autism,
but sometimes plans can, and need to be, changed. When I was little,
my nanny made my sister and me do a variety of activities. This variety prevented rigid behavior patterns from forming. I became more
accustomed to changes in our daily or weekly routines and learned that
I could still manage when change occurred. This same principle
applies to animals. Cattle that are always fed from the red truck by Jim
may panic if Sally pulls up in a white truck to feed them. To prevent
this problem, progressive ranchers have learned to alter routines
slightly so that cattle learn to accept some variation.

Another way to teach flexibility of thinking is to use visual metaphors, such as mixing paint. To understand complex situations, such as when occasionally a good friend does something nasty, I imagine mixing white and black paint. If the friend's behavior is mostly nice, the mixture is a very light gray; if the person is really not a friend then the mixture is a very dark gray.

Flexibility can also be taught by showing the person with autism that categories can change. Objects can be sorted by color, function, or material. To test this idea, I grabbed a bunch of black, red, and yellow objects in my office and laid them on the floor. They were a stapler, a roll of tape, a ball, videotapes, a toolbox, a hat, and pens. Depending upon the situation, any of these objects could be used for either work or play. Ask the child to give concrete examples of using a stapler for work or play. For instance, stapling office papers is work; stapling a kite together is play. Simple situations like this that teach a child flexibility in thinking and relating can be found numerous times in each day.

Children do need to be taught that some rules apply everywhere and should not be broken. To teach an autistic child to not run across the street, he has to be taught the rule in many different places; the rule has to be generalized and part of that process is making sure the child understands that the rule should not be broken. However, there are times when an absolute adherence to the rule can cause harm. Children also need to be taught that some rules can change depending on the situation. Emergencies are one such category where rules may be allowed to be broken.

Parents, teachers and therapists can continually teach and reinforce flexible thinking patterns in children with autism/AS. I hope I have provided some ideas on how to do this while still accommodating the visual manner in which they think.

Teaching Concepts to Children with Autism

G ENERALLY, PEOPLE WITH AUTISM POSSESS GOOD SKILLS IN LEARN-
ing rules, but they can have less developed abstract thinking
skills. Dr. Nancy Minshew and her colleagues at the University of
Pittsburgh have done research that may help teachers understand how
the autistic mind thinks. For the autistic, learning rules is easy, but
learning flexibility in thinking is difficult, and must be taught.

There are three basic levels of conceptual thinking: 1) learning rules
2) identifying categories, and 3) inventing new categories. Category-
forming ability can be tested by placing a series of objects on a table,
such as pencils, notepads, cups, nail files, paper clips, napkins, bottles,
videotapes, and other common objects. A person with autism can easily identify all the pencils, or all the bottles. He can also easily identify
objects in simple categories, such as all the objects that are green or all
the metal objects. Conceptual thinking at this basic level is generally
not a problem.

Where the person with autism has extreme difficulty is inventing
new categories, which is the beginning of true concept formation. For
example, many of the objects in the list referenced above could be clas-
sified by use (i.e., office supplies) or by shape (round/not round). To
me, it is obvious that a cup, a bottle and a pencil are all round. Most
people would classify a video cassette as not-round; however, I might
put it into the round category because of its round spools inside.

39

One of the easiest ways to teach concept formation is through playing category-forming games with children. For example, a cup can be used to drink from, or to store pencils or paper clips. In one situation, it is used for drinking; the other it is used in the office or at work. A videotape can be used for recreation or education, depending on the content the tape. Notepads can be used for note taking, for art drawings, or, more abstractly, as a paperweight or a coaster for a glass. Activities such as these must be done with a high degree of repetition; it will take some time for the person with autism to learn to think differently. However, with perseverance, results will occur.

Helping children "get into their head" different and varied ways of categorizing objects is the first step in developing flexible thinking. The more examples provided, the more flexible his or her thinking can become. The more flexible the thinking, the easier it will be for the person with autism to learn to develop new categories and concepts. Once the child has acquired some flexible thinking skills with concrete objects, teachers can begin to expand their conceptual thinking into the less concrete areas of categorizing feelings, emotions, facial expressions, etc.

Flexibility of thinking is a highly important ability that is often—to the detriment of the child—omitted as a teachable skill on a child's IEP. It impacts a child in all environments, both now and in the future: school, home, relationships, employment, recreation. Parents and teachers need to give it more attention when developing a child's educational plan.

REFERENCE

Minshew, N.J., J. Meyer, and G. Goldstein. 2002. Abstract reasoning in autism: A dissociation between concept formation and concept identification. *Neurospychology* 16: 327-334.

Motivating
Students

ONE FREQUENT CHARACTERISTIC OF INDIVIDUALS ON THE AUTISM/ Asperger's spectrum is an obsessive interest in one or a few particular subjects, to the exclusion of others. These individuals may be near-genius on a topic of interest, even at a very early age. Parents have described to me their ten-year-old child whose knowledge of electricity rivals that of a college senior, or a near-teen whose knowledge of insects far surpasses that of his biology teacher. However, as motivated as they are to study what they enjoy, these students are often equally unmotivated when it comes to school work outside their area of interest.

It was like this with me when I was in high school. I was totally unmotivated about school work in general. But I was highly motivated to work on the things that interested me, such as showing horses, painting signs, and carpentry projects. Luckily, my mother and some of my teachers used my special interests to keep me motivated. Mr. Carlock, my science teacher, took my obsessive interests in cattle chutes and the squeeze machine to motivate me in studying science. The squeeze machine relaxed me. Mr. Carlock told me that if I really wanted to know why the machine had this effect, I would have to study the boring school subjects so that I could graduate and then go to college to become a scientist who could answer this question. Once I really grasped the idea that to get from here to there—from middle school to graduation to college and then to a job of interest to me—I needed to apply myself to all my school subjects, boring or not. This understanding maintained my motivation to complete the work.

While students are in elementary school, teachers can easily keep them involved by using a special interest to motivate their learning. An example would be taking a student's interest in trains and using a train theme in many different subjects. In history class, read about the history of the railroad; in math class, involve trains in problem solving; in science class, discuss different forms of energy that trains utilized then and now, etc.

As students move into middle and high school, they can get turned on by visiting interesting work places, such as a construction site, an architecture firm, or a research lab. This makes the idea of a career real to the student and they begin to understand the education path they must take early on in school to achieve that career. If visiting a work site is not possible, invite parents who have interesting jobs into the school classroom to talk with students about their jobs. Lots of pictures to show what the work is like are strongly recommended. This is also an opportunity for students to hear about the social side of employment, which can provide motivation for making new friends, joining groups or venturing out into social situations that might be uncomfortable at first.

Students on the spectrum need to be exposed to new things in order to become interested in them. They need to see concrete examples of really cool things to keep them motivated to learn. I became fascinated by optical illusions after seeing a single movie in science class that demonstrated optical illusions. My science teacher challenged me to recreate two famous optical illusions, called the Ames Distorted Room and the Ames Trapezoidal Window. I spent six months making them out of cardboard and plywood and I finally figured them out. This motivated me to study experimental psychology in college.

Bring Trade Magazines to the Library

Scientific journals, trade magazines, and business newspapers can show students a wide range of careers and help turn students on to the opportunities available after they graduate. Every profession from the most complex to the practical has its trade journal. Trade magazines are published in fields as diverse as banking, baking, car wash operation, construction, building maintenance, electronics, and many others. Parents who already work in these fields could bring their old trade journals to the school library. These magazines would provide a window into the world of jobs and help motivate students.

If my third grade teacher had
continued trying to teach me
to read with endless, boring drills,
I would have failed the
reading competency tests required
by No Child Left Behind.

✯

Getting Kids Turned On to Reading

ONE COMPLAINT I AM HEARING FROM BOTH PARENTS AND TEACHERS is that the No Child Left Behind law makes it impossible to spend much time on subjects other than reading and math because school districts put so much emphasis on students passing tests in these subjects. Recently, I had a discussion with a mom about teaching reading. She told me that her daughter, who has reading problems, was not allowed to go outside for recess because she had to do reading drills. The girl was bored stiff and hated it. However, she quickly learned to read when her mom taught her from a Harry Potter book. To motivate kids, especially those with autism spectrum disorders, you need to start with books the kids want to read. The Harry Potter series is one of the best things that has happened to reading instruction. Two hours before the last Harry Potter book went on sale, I visited the local Barnes and Noble. It was jammed full of kids in costume and a line stretched half way around the block. I think it is wonderful that the kids were getting so turned on about a book.

I could not read when I was in third grade. Mother taught me to read after school from an interesting book about Clara Barton, a famous nurse. The content kept me interested, and motivated me to learn, even though the book was written at the sixth grade level.

Mother taught me how to sound out the words, and within three months, my reading skills jumped two grade levels on standardized tests. I was a phonics learner, but other kids on the autism spectrum are visual, sight-word learners. When they read the word *dog*, they see a picture of a dog in their head. Children are different; parents should identify which way their child learns best and then use that method.

Sight-word readers usually learn nouns first. To learn the meaning of words like *went* and *going* I had to see them in a sentence I could visualize. For example, "I *went* to the supermarket" or "I am *going* to the supermarket." One is past and the other is future. When I *went* to the supermarket I see myself with the bag of groceries I purchased. When I say I am *going* to the supermarket, I see myself driving there. Use examples the child can visualize and relate to when teaching all the connector words that are not easily visualized themselves.

If my third grade teacher had continued trying to teach me to read with endless, boring drills, I would have failed the reading competency tests required by No Child Left Behind. After mother taught me reading, I was able to do really well on the elementary school reading tests. She got me engaged in reading in a way that was meaningful to me until reading became naturally reinforcing on its own.

Parents and teachers can use a child's special interests or natural talents in creative ways to teach basic academic skills such as reading and math. Science and history make wonderfully interesting topics to teach both subjects to spectrum children. If the child likes dinosaurs, teach reading using books about dinosaurs. A simple math problem might be rewritten using dinosaurs as the subject or new exercises created by the adult. For example: if a dinosaur walks at five miles per hour, how far can he walk in fifteen minutes?

Students with ASD can get excellent scores on standardized tests when more creative methods are used that appeal to their interests and ways of thinking. Although this creative effort may take a little more time at the onset, the improved learning, interest and motivation in the child will more than make up for the extra time in the long run.

The Importance
of Practical
Problem-Solving Skills

B OTH NORMAL CHILDREN AND KIDS ON THE AUTISM SPECTRUM NEED to be challenged. Those who have heard me speak or read my books know I think many parents and educators coddle their children with ASD far more than they should. Children with ASD don't belong in a bubble, sheltered from the normal experiences of the world around them. Sensory issues do need to be taken into consideration, but aside from those, parents may need to push their child a little for any real advancement in learning to occur.

This is especially true in teaching a pivotal life skill: problem-solving. It involves training the brain to be organized, break down tasks into step-by-step sequences, relate parts to the whole, stay on task, and experience a sense of personal accomplishment once the problem is solved.

Young kids learn by doing, and kids with ASD often learn best with concrete, visible examples. When I was a child growing up in the '50s, I built tree houses and went on backyard campouts with other neighborhood children. In those situations, several children had to work together to figure out how to accomplish the task. We had to find lumber for the tree house, design it, and take measurements, and discuss how to get the boards up the tree and nailed into place. We learned by trying different things; some things worked, others did not.

Experiments with wetting lumber to make it easier to cut with a hand saw were a complete failure. From our experiences, we learned that dry lumber was easier to cut.

The rigorous turn-taking training I had when I was 3-6 years old served me well in these group activities. In our family we played lots of board games—an excellent teaching method for learning how to take turns. Turn-taking helped me understand that people can work together for a common purpose, that what one person did could affect me and the outcome of the game positively or negatively. It made me aware of different perspectives, which in turn helped me become a better detective when I had to solve a problem.

I can remember the huge planning meetings we had for the backyard campout. There was candy and soda that had to be bought. We all had to figure out how to put up an old army tent. None of the parents helped, which made it a valuable learning experience for us all.

Like myself, many kids with ASD have a natural curiosity about certain things. These interests can be used constructively to practice problem-solving skills. I loved toys that flew. On a windy day, a parachute I made from a scarf would fly for hundreds of feet. But not on the first try. It took many attempts before I was successful. I had to figure out how to prevent the strings from tangling when I threw the parachute up into the air. I tried building a cross from two pieces of 5" coat-hanger wire to tie the four strings to; it worked. When I was in high school, I was fascinated with optical illusions. After seeing an illusion called the Ames Trapezoidal Window, I wanted to build one. My science teacher challenged me to try to figure it out by myself rather than giving me a book with a diagram. I spent six months working on it, without success. Then my teacher let me have a brief glimpse at a photo in a textbook that showed how the illusion worked. He gave me a hint without telling me exactly how to do it. He helped me develop problem-solving skills.

Children with ASD (and many of their parents) struggle with problem-solving skills today. This may be partially due to us, as a society, doing less hands-on practical work and activities than did our counterparts when I was growing up. We fix less; we toss things out that don't work and buy new. Even in today's internet world, there is a need for problem-solving skills. The key is to start with concrete, hands-on projects that have meaning for the child, then slowly move into abstract problem-solving involving thoughts and creativity, in academics and social situations. The ability to solve problems helps a person categorize and use the vast amounts of information in his mind, and from outside sources like the internet, in a successful, intelligent manner. These are important life skills and parents should start early in incorporating problem-solving opportunities into their child's daily routine.

Remember a basic principle
in working with autistic individuals:
an obsession or fixation
holds huge motivation
potential to the child.

✦

Turning Video Game Obsessions into Learning

I'M A FIRM BELIEVER THAT THERE ARE CERTAIN CHARACTERISTICS OF autism and Asperger's that can be used to a person's advantage, if channeled in the right way by the parents and educators involved with the child. One of these characteristics is the obsessive interest children often have in things. Parents ask me all the time: how do I help my child become interested in learning when all he wants to do is play video games or draw Japanese anime cartoons? My response is this: turn that video game obsession into learning opportunities!

Often the most effective method is to use elements of the game or the cartoons that can be applied to other activities. Many popular games are based on a quest for a goal. Inspire a child to read by explaining that there exist great works of literature about quests that have similarities to those in a video game. King Arthur and his knights of the Round Table were on a quest. Another example might be taking a child's Superman fixation and using it to motivate learning in math and science. For example, how long would it take Superman to fly across the U.S. at the speed of sound?

The Mario video games center around a character who is a plumber. This could be used in a way to start an interest in plumbing or to practice problem-solving skills. You could ask the child, "What does Mario do when he is not in the video game? He fixes pipes." Or ask the child to connect different sizes and shapes of pipe to get from location A to

B, or use different plumbing supplies as sorting objects, or to hone math skills.

If a child spends hours drawing the same cartoon over and over again, use that obsession as the starting point to broaden the subject matter of the drawings. Instead of endless pictures of Mickey Mouse, you might suggest drawing Mickey's house or Mickey's car. To channel the huge motivation the fixation provides into a new direction, there must be a direct association between the existing fixation and the new request. As the child's mind becomes more flexible, you can broaden the associations into other areas that address new skills. For instance, after drawing Mickey's house, suggest drawing Mickey eating dinner, then Mickey setting the table or Mickey helping Mom prepare dinner.

For some children, video games border on obsessions because of the visual stimulation they hold. If video games had been available when I was growing up, I would have been addicted to them if I had been allowed to play them all day; I loved watching rapid movement. (Mother would never have permitted that.) While there are some children who have the skills to become successful video game programmers, I am not one of them. The games would have been a distraction from learning other skills I needed. In my case, I would have spent my time playing video games instead of developing my talents in building things. I might have ended up unemployable instead of becoming as successful as I am today.

The way I see it, video game playing should be limited to an hour per day, or some other finite amount of time that is reasonable for the individual. If left unchecked, true obsessions can prevent a child from engaging in other activities that will benefit his learning and development in the long run. Parents need to step in and be firm in curbing obsessions by transforming them into more productive activities in the child's life. This may be difficult at first, with much resistance on the part of the child—especially if he has been allowed free reign in his obsessions for months or years. He may not understand why it was okay to play these games as much as he wanted before and now it is no longer so. Parents must be patient and creative in how they approach this situation, and gradually reduce the time spent on video games while stimulating interest in other activities by using the game components as the bridge between the two.

Remember a basic principle in working with autistic individuals: an obsession or fixation holds huge motivation potential to the child. Video games are one such fixation shared by many individuals on the spectrum. He will work at learning new things or new activities to gain access to his video games. Use that to your advantage to help him grow and expand his understanding of the world beyond that of hand-held games.

Sensory
Issues

Chapter

3

Visual Processing Problems in Autism

Auditory Problems in Autism

Incorporating Sensory Integration into Your Autism Program

The Effect of Sensory Perceptual Difficulties on Learning Styles

✸

One of the problems in understanding sensory issues is that sensory sensitivities are very variable, among individuals and within the same individual.

I HAVE BEEN TALKING AND WRITING ABOUT SENSORY PROBLEMS FOR over twenty years and I am still perplexed by many people who do not acknowledge sensory issues and the pain and discomfort they can cause. A person doesn't have to be on the autism spectrum to be affected by sensory issues. Most people feel an aversion to nails being drawn across a chalkboard. That's a negative sensory experience. Many times I have heard of people who get almost instant headaches when exposed to certain scents, like strong perfumes or the smell of gasoline. That's a sensory experience. A woman I know tells me her hearing is very sensitive when she first wakes up in the morning, and even normal sounds are sometimes offensive for the first thirty minutes or so. That's a sensory challenge. Think about going to the mall and shopping on a busy Saturday afternoon. For some it's energizing, but for others, it leaves them exhausted. These people are having trouble with the sensory bombardments that are typical of the mall environment: the constantly changing sights, smells, voices and music, being bumped by others, etc. Sensory issues are very real, and I think they are more a matter of degree than being either present or absent in people. I also believe that as our world in general gets louder and busier with more people, more cars, more urbanization, and a heavier reliance on technology, sensory issues are more and more pervasive as our sensory systems become increasingly overloaded.

For me, and other people on the autism spectrum, sensory experiences that have little or no effect on neurotypical people can be severe life stressors for us. Loud noises hurt my ears like a dentist's drill hitting a nerve. For some individuals, the seams in a pair of socks or the rough texture of materials like wool can feel like being constantly burned. This explains why a child's reaction is to take them off—he's not being defiant; the socks are physically hurting him. For others, even the light touch of another's hand on their arm can be painful. They shrink away from people not because they are unsocial, but because even brushing up against another person can feel like razors drawn across their skin.

I think so many professionals and nonprofessionals have ignored sensory issues because some people just can't imagine that an alternate sensory reality exists if they have not experienced it personally. They simply cannot imagine it, so it does not register in their minds. That type of narrow perception, however, does nothing to help individuals who do have these very real issues in their lives. Even if they don't understand it on a personal level, it's time they put aside their personal ideas. Scientific research has now documented that sensory problems are real. Higher functioning adults with autism and Asperger's are writing about their sensory issues in great detail. Many of these individuals agree that sensory issues are the primary challenge the autism presents them in their daily lives. There is a great need for more scientific research on the brain abnormalities that are associated with different sensory problems and methods to treat them.

Sensory Problems are Variable

One of the problems in understanding sensory issues is that sensory sensitivities are very variable, among individuals and within the same individual. A person can be hyper-sensitive in one area (like hearing) and hypo-sensitive in another (like touch). One person can have a marked olfactory sensitivity and another might not be affected at all in that sense. Complicating matters even further, on a day-to-day basis, in the same individual, the sensory sensitivities can change, especially when the child is tired or stressed. These many and constantly shifting variables make it difficult to design research studies to test therapies to treat sensory sensitivities. So professionals will loudly make assertions such as "There is no research to support sensory integration therapy with individuals with autism"—tacitly suggesting the therapy is ineffective. The absence of clinical research does not mean sensory therapies are not viable for children or adults. It simply means research has not been done to date. Furthermore, with the variable nature of sensory issues in autism, we must look at research with a slightly different slant. If twenty children are put in a study and four benefit from the therapy, while sixteen don't, is it ethical to deem the therapy ineffective? It really worked on four children. For four children, their lives are now markedly different; their world is no longer hellish to live within. A better approach in situations like this is to delve deeper into why it works for some and not for others, to continue to explore what is going on in their brains by doing follow-up research between the responders and non-responders, rather than arbitrarily dismissing the therapy altogether.

Parents and teachers often ask—"How can I tell if my child has sensory problems?" My simple answer is this: watch your child closely—the signs are there. Do you see him putting his hands over his ears to block out noise? Does he become agitated every time you're in a bustling, noisy, or chaotic environment? Are there certain textures of food he just will not tolerate? Do you find her pulling at or taking off clothes that have rough textures or tugging at necklines where tags are rubbing? Children and adults who tantrum and cannot tolerate being in a large supermarket, such as Wal-Mart, are almost certain to have sensory problems. Also note: tolerance levels quickly diminish when the individual is tired or hungry. A child may tolerate a large grocery store in the morning but not during the afternoon.

Easy Strategies

There are some simple things parents, educators and service providers can do to help prevent sensory problems from hindering your child's education and life. Avoid multi-tasking, especially when working with the child. Have a quiet place free from outside distractions to do teaching, discrete trials, or other therapies. I have difficulty hearing if there is too much background noise—I can't discern my communication partner's voice from all the other sounds going on around me. Make sure the child gets lots of exercise every day. A significant number of research studies support the benefits of regular daily exercise. Exercise is really good for the brain and can help children with hyper sensitivities calm down, and children with hypo-sensitivities rev up their system for optimal learning states. One of the articles in this section discusses simple ways to incorporate calming sensory activities into an educational program.

Sometimes very simple interventions can have amazing effects, as is described in the article on visual processing problems. One little girl could not tolerate a large supermarket for more than five minutes. After her mother bought her a pair of children's tinted pink sunglasses, she was able to get through an hour of shopping. Other children learn better when they are shielded from the distracting flicker of fluorescent lights. Some of the energy-saver fluorescent light bulbs have such a high degree of flicker that I cannot read with them. Some fluorescent lamps have electronic circuits to reduce flicker, but others make some people on the autism spectrum feel like they are standing in the middle of a disco nightclub. (Try concentrating on a test within that type of environment!) If fluorescent lights cannot be avoided, a lamp with an old fashioned incandescent light bulb should be placed next to the child's desk to help eliminate flickers, or kids can wear baseball caps with longer brims to mask off some of the flicker.

Auditory Problems

Auditory challenges are often cited as the #1 sensory challenge among individuals with autism/Asperger's. There are two kinds of auditory problems: 1) sensitivity to loud noise in general and 2) not being able to hear auditory detail such as discerning one voice among other sounds, or hearing the hard consonant sounds of words. An auditory sensitivity to noises, where sounds hurt the ears, can be extremely debilitating. Sound sensitivity can make it **impossible** for some people on the spectrum to tolerate normal places such as restaurants, offices, and sports events. These extreme auditory problems can occur in both nonverbal individuals and those who are very high-functioning with marked intelligences and language capabilities, like college-educated people with Asperger's.

Auditory training therapy is useful for some people. In auditory training, a person listens to electronically distorted music a couple of sessions a day for ten days. The music sounds like an old-fashioned record player that is speeding up and slowing down. AT helps some children and adults, yet has no effect on others. The main improvements seen in those that it helps include reducing sound sensitivity and improving hearing of auditory detail. For many children, getting their auditory input under control results in improved concentration, fewer behavior issues, and gives a chance for other therapies and learning situations to take hold. Some people with more minor auditory challenges use earplugs or music headphones to block out distracting or hurtful sounds, things such as chairs scraping on the floor in the cafeteria, the constant ringing of telephones in a busy office, or maneuvering through a crowded airport. Ear plugs must never be worn all the time; this can cause the individual to become even more sensitive to sound. They need to be off at least half of the day but can be used in noisy places such as shopping malls or the gym.

An Integrated Approach to Treatment

Severe sensory sensitivity can be a MAJOR barrier to learning in children, and in employment and socializing as the child grows and becomes an adult. My own sensory problems are minor nuisances, but for others, they can literally wreck the person's life. There are many highly intelligent adults with Asperger's, with brilliant minds in their field, who have such severe sensory issues that they cannot tolerate a normal job environment. They must either find ways to work independently from home, where they can control sensory input, or remain largely unemployed. Employers are beginning to understand sensory issues and some will even make accommodations when the needs of the person are explained. However, on the whole, we as a society have far to go in appreciating the challenge of living with sensory issues that most people on the autism spectrum face daily.

Teachers and parents should look closely for sensory issues in a child or young adult. Recurring behavior problems often have a sensory issue as the root cause of the behavior. If a sensory issue is suspected, a consultation with a good Occupational Therapist should be the next step. These individuals are trained to recognize sensory issues and then develop a customized program for the child. Interventions such as deep pressure, slow swinging, and games involving balancing work best when they are done every day.

Sensory issues are daily issues. If the services of an OT are available for only half an hour each week, parents and teachers should visit the session and ask the OT to show them what to do the rest of the week. For children, a combination of sensory therapies such as sensory integration from an OT, auditory training, and visual interventions coupled with other treatments works best. Special diets help some children with their sensory issues; improvements are seen not just in tolerating different textures and types of food, but also in other sensory areas as well. With older children and adults, a little dose of a conventional medication may reduce sound sensitivity if less invasive methods have proven unsuccessful.

ADDITIONAL READING

Ayres, J.A. 1979. *Sensory integration and the child.* Los Angeles, CA: Western Psychological Press.

Blackmore, S.J. et al. 2006. Tactile sensitivity in Asperger syndrome. *Brain and Cognition* 61: 5-13.

Cascio, C. et al. 2008. Tactile perception in adults with autism: A multidimensional psychophysical study. *Journal of Autism and Developmental Disorders* 38: 127-137.

Cotman, C.W., N.C. Berhtold, and L.A. Christie. 2007. Exercise builds brain health: Key roles of growth factor cascades and inflammation. *Trends in Neuroscience* 30: 464-472.

Edelson, S.M., M.G. Edelson, D.C. Kerr, and T. Grandin. 1999. Behavioral and physiological effects of deep pressure in children with autism: A pilot study evaluating the efficacy of Grandin's Hug Machine. *American Journal of Occupational Therapy* 53: 145-152.

Evans, B.J., and F. Joseph. 2002. The effect of coloured filters on the rate of reading in an adult student population. *Ophthalmic Physiological Optometry* 19: 274-285.

Grandin, T. 2006. *Thinking in pictures* (Expanded Edition). New York: Vintage/Random House.

Leekam, S.R., C. Nieto, S.J. Libby, L. Wing, and J. Gould. 2007. Describing the sensory abnormalities of children and adults with autism. *Journal of Autism and Developmental Disorders* 37: 894-910.

Lightstone, A., T. Lightstone, and A. Wilkins. 1999. Both coloured overlays and coloured lenses improve reading fluency but these optimal chromaticities differ. *Ophthalmic Physiological Optometry* 19: 274-285.

Miller, L.C. 2006. *Sensational kids: Hope and help for children with sensory processing disorder.* New York: G.P. Putnam/Penguin Group.

Minshew, N.J., and J.A. Hobson. 2008. Sensory sensitivities and performance on sensory perceptual tasks in high-functioning individuals with autism. *Journal of Autism and Developmental Disorders* (in press).

Ray, T.C., L.J. King, and T. Grandin. 1988. The effectiveness of self-initiated vestibular stimulation in producing speech sounds. *Journal of Occupational Therapy* 8: 186-190.

A child who can see his world
clearly has a much better chance
of benefiting from other therapies.

✫

Visual Processing
Problems in Autism

VISUAL PROCESSING PROBLEMS ARE COMMON IN INDIVIDUALS WITH autism spectrum disorders. They can result in lack of eye contact, staring at objects, or using side vision. These individuals may have difficulty with visually "holding still"—they constantly scan their surroundings for visual information in an attempt to gain meaning.

Suspect a visual processing problem if you see an autistic child tilt his head and look out of the corner of his eye. Children or adults with visual processing difficulties can see flicker in fluorescent lights and they may have difficulty going up and down stairs because of distorted depth perception. Most normal children love to play on escalators, but a child with poor vision processing may fear the escalator. Some children and adults may have difficulty reading because black print on a white page will jiggle and vibrate. Adults with mild vision processing problems may hate driving at night.

Donna Williams, a well-known high-functioning person with autism, often described her visual processing problems. Faces appeared like two-dimensional Picasso-like mosaics. High-contrasting colors in room décor were distressing. Other individuals have complained that yellow and black caution stripes appear to vibrate. Motor, cognitive, speech, and perceptual abilities can all be affected when visual processing is interrupted.

A regular eye exam will not find these problems. To correctly diagnose and treat visual processing problems, a developmental optometrist should be consulted. Recently I attended the annual convention of COVD—the College of Optometrists in Vision Development—and I was amazed at the array of therapies that are available. Some of the most common are colored glasses, prism lenses, and computer-based eye exercises.

Many people have been helped by wearing Irlen colored glasses. It is best to be tested by a professional and it is essential that the person be allowed to choose the color that works best for him or her. Many people with limited incomes have discovered that lightly tinted sunglasses can lessen their visual distortion, making reading easier and allowing them to better tolerate rooms with high contrasting décor. Usually the pinkish, purplish to brown tints work best. Sunglass stores now have many tinted lenses that are in more appropriate lighter tints. Take a book into the store and try reading with different colored lens. Another helpful aid is printing reading materials on tan, gray, or pastel paper to reduce contrast. A laptop computer has less screen flicker and is often easier on the eyes than is a TV-type monitor. A flat panel monitor is also good but make sure it does not have a fluorescent light inside.

Autistic individuals can also ignore peripheral vision (side vision) and remain fixated on a central point of focus for excessive periods of time. People with very sensitive visual processing problems are often nonverbal and they may be seeing the world as if they were looking through two toilet paper tubes. Their visual field around the tubes may look like a kaleidoscope, with only the very center area clear visually. To see properly they have to tilt their head or move the object into the their sphere of vision.

Dr. Melvin Kaplan and Steve Edelson have found that prism glasses can help some individuals with autism. Prism glasses are clear glass lenses slightly thicker at the top or bottom; they should be prescribed by a developmental optometrist. This specialist also can prescribe eye exercises and vision training activities.

Due to the high variability within autism spectrum disorders, not all individuals will benefit from vision therapy. However, a child who can see his world clearly has a much better chance of benefiting from other therapies.

FOR FURTHER INFORMATION VISIT THE FOLLOWING WEBSITES:

The Irlen Institute, *www.irlen.com*

College of Optometrists in Vision Development, *www.covd.org*

Optometric Extension Program Foundation: *www.oep.org*; click on "Resource Center"

Dr. Melvin Kaplan's site, *www.autisticvision.com*

REFERENCES

Kaplan, M., S.M. Edelson, and J.L. Seip. 1998. Behavioral changes in autistic individuals as a result of wearing ambient transitional prism lenses. *Child Psychiatry and Human Development* 29:65-67.

Lightstone, A., T. Lightstone, and A. Wilkins. 1999. Both coloured overlays and coloured lenses can improve reading fluency, but their optimal chromaticities differ. *Ophthalmic and Physiological Optics* 4: 279-285.

Wilkins, A. 2002. Coloured overlays and their effects on reading speed: A review. *Ophthalmic and Physiological Optics* 5: 448-454.

When I was little, I could understand
what people were saying when
they spoke directly to me,
but when adults talked fast,
it sounded like gibberish.

⋆

Auditory Problems
in Autism

ANYONE WHO HAS ATTENDED ONE OF MY PRESENTATIONS KNOWS that it is my opinion that sensory issues are a big part of behavior problems in children with autism. I, myself, have many sensory issues, and one that affects me the most is hearing/sound.

When I was a child, the ringing of the school bell hurt my ears; it felt like a dentist's drill hitting a nerve. This is common among the autism population. The sounds that are most likely to hurt the ears are high-pitched shrill, intermittent sounds, such as fire alarms, smoke detectors, certain ring tones on mobile phones, or the screech of feedback from a microphone. Once a child experiences the pain associated with certain sounds, he is not soon to forget it. Subsequently, a child may have a tantrum and refuse to enter a certain room because he may be afraid that the fire alarm might go off, or that the assembly microphone might screech again. Even if it happened months and months ago, and even if it only happened one time he may take action to avoid feeling that pain again. Sometimes sound sensitivity can be desensitized by recording the offending sound and allowing the child to initiate the sound at gradually increasing volume. Problems with sound sensitivity are very variable. A sound that hurts the ears of one child may be attractive to another. Parents and professionals need to be good detectives and watch for clues from the child about what auditory sounds are troublesome.

Auditory Detail

Even though children and adults with ASD can easily pass a standard hearing test, they often have difficulty with hearing auditory detail. When I was little, I could understand what people were saying when they spoke directly to me, but when adults talked fast, it sounded like gibberish. All I could hear were the vowels and I thought that grown-ups had their own "grown-up" language. Children who remain nonverbal may be hearing only the vowels and no consonants.

My speech teacher helped me hear the consonants by stretching them out. She would hold up a cup and ask me to say "c-c-c—u—p-p-p." She alternated between saying "cup" the normal way and stretching it out. If there was a lot of background noise I had difficulty hearing. Eye contact is still difficult for me in noisy rooms because it interferes with hearing. It's like my brain wiring lets only one sense function or the other but sometimes not both at the same time. In noisy rooms, I have to concentrate on hearing.

As an adult I took a number of central auditory processing tests and was shocked at how poorly I did. Words like "life boat" and "light bulb" were mixed up. I did poorly on the dichotic listening test where I had a man talking in one ear and a woman talking in the other ear. When I had to attend to my left ear, I was functionally deaf. However, both of my ears tested normal in the simple hearing threshold test. I also had difficulty discriminating between two short sounds that occurred close together. For example, a one-second sound followed by a half-second gap and then another one-second sound is perceived as a single sound. Normal people can discriminate which sound has a higher pitch, and therefore their brain registers two sounds. I cannot do this because the sounds blend together.

Parents and teachers working with children with ASD need to be aware of these auditory processing difficulties. Sometimes a child's behavior can be a direct result of his or her lack of auditory processing skills, rather than disobedience or what may look like "acting out" behaviors. Imagine how you would (or would not) function if you only heard parts of words, only vowels, or only certain tones. How much important, relevant information would you miss every day, every hour, every minute?

A child who has difficulty hearing auditory detail will benefit from the use of visual supports, such as written words on flash cards, written instructions, or written homework assignments. He may need to hear and read the word at the same time for comprehension to take place.

REFERENCES

Johansson, O., and D. Lindegreen. 2008. Analysis of everyday sounds which are extremely annoying for children with autism. *Journal of Acoustical Society of America* 123: 3299.

Heaton, P., R.E. Davis, and F.G. Happe. 2008. Research note: Exceptional absolute pitch perception for spoken words in an able adult with autism. *Neuropsychologia* 46: 2095-2098.

Sensory integration activities
may help unscramble the child's
perception and enable information
to get through–a prerequisite
for any type of learning.

Incorporating Sensory Integration into your Autism Program

C HILDREN AND ADULTS WITH AUTISM SPECTRUM DISORDERS, BE they mildly or severely challenged, have one or more of their senses affected to the extent that it interferes with their ability to learn and process information from the world around them. Often, the sense of hearing is the most affected, but vision, touch, taste, smell, balance (vestibular), and awareness of their body in space (proprioception) can all function abnormally in the person with autism. Therefore, I am a strong proponent of sensory integration (SI) as a must-have therapy for this population.

It is just common sense that sensory integration activities such as relaxing deep pressure, swinging, visual tools, and other strategies be components of any good autism program. These activities help the child's nervous system calm down so the child can be more receptive to learning. They can help reduce hyperactivity, tantrums, and repetitive stimming, or rev up a lagging system in a child who is hypo-sensitive. SI assures that a child is at optimal levels of attention and readiness to benefit from other intervention programs, such as behavioral, educational, speech, or social skills programs.

To be effective, sensory activities must be done every day. I still encounter parents and some professionals who believe that SI doesn't work, precisely because the activities have to be repeated on a daily basis. Would you question whether or not eyeglasses worked because they had to be used every day? Another example is using medication to improve behaviors. Medication has to be taken every day in order for it to be effective. The same holds true for sensory activities.

ABA (Applied Behavior Analysis) techniques are the core of many good autism programs. Research clearly shows that a good ABA program using discrete trial is very effective for teaching language to young children with ASD. The best ABA programs carried out today are more flexible than the original Lovaas method, where most of the activities were done while the child was seated at a table. Newer programs have a greater variety of activities, and teaching often takes place in more natural settings. However, even well-trained ABA professionals are frequently bewildered with incorporating SI into their behavior-based program. In my opinion, their problem stems from them viewing SI (or any adjunct therapy program) as separate and apart from the ABA program. Therapies for children with autism are interrelated. We can't work just on behavior, or just on social skills, or just on sensory. The progress achieved in one area will affect functioning in another, and all need to be integrated into a whole to achieve maximum benefits. To use a visual analogy: a good ABA program is like a Christmas tree. It is the framework, the foundation, the base of a child's therapeutic program. Because of the differences that people on the spectrum manifest, other adjunct programs are often needed in addition to ABA, like sensory integration, dietary intervention, social skills training, or language therapy. These services are the ornaments on the tree, which render each tree unique, beautiful, and specific to one child's needs and level of functioning.

There are several easy ways to integrate sensory integration into a young child's behavior-based program. Try doing some discrete trials while the child receives soothing pressure. One child I knew learned best when he lay across a beanbag chair, and another bag was placed on top of him, sandwich style. The pressure calmed his nervous system and made him ready for learning. Try slow swinging—ten to twelve times a minute—during the lesson. Swinging helps stimulate language and is why a growing number of speech and occupational therapists hold joint therapy sessions to improve learning. To help a fidgety child sit still and attend to his lesson, try a weighted vest. The vest is most effective if the child wears it for twenty minutes and then takes it off for twenty minutes. This prevents habituation. Conversely, rev up a slower sensory system so that learning can happen by doing a drill while a child jumps on a trampoline, or by using a vibrating chair pad.

Some of the children with the most severe autism function like a TV with bad reception: visual and auditory perception fade in and out depending on the strength of the signal. In the most severe cases, visual and auditory information is scrambled, rendering the child unable to decipher what he sees or hears at any given moment. Recent brain scan studies show that the brain circuits that perceive complex sounds are abnormal. Sensory integration activities may help unscramble the child's perception and enable information to get through—a prerequisite for any type of learning.

While sensory challenges often lessen over time, and especially as a result of SI treatment, we must acknowledge the detrimental effects that sensory impairments have on the ability of children with ASD to benefit from any treatment, and plan accordingly. Sensory integration should be an important part of any treatment program for a person with ASD.

REFERENCES

Boddart, N. et al. 2004. Perception of complex sounds in autism: Abnormal auditory cortical processing in children. *American Journal of Psychiatry* 161: 2117-2120.

Ray, T.C., L.J. King, and T. Grandin. 1988. The effectiveness of self-initiated vestibular stimulation on producing speech sounds. *Journal of Occupational Therapy Research* 8: 186-190.

Smith, S.A., B. Press, K.P. Koenig, and M. Kinnealey. 2005. Effects of sensory integration intervention on self-stimulating and self-injurious behaviors. *America Journal of Occupational Therapy* 59: 418-425.

Zisserman, L. 1992. The effect of deep pressure on self-stimulating behaviors in a child with autism and other disabilities. *American Journal of Occupational Therapy* 46: 547-551.

The Effect of Sensory
and Perceptual Difficulties
on Learning Styles

INDIVIDUALS ON THE AUTISM SPECTRUM HAVE REMARKABLY VARIED problems with sensory over-sensitivity and information processing. While these problems originate in the brain—their source is biological—they manifest in behaviors that compromise the individuals' ability to learn and function in the world around them. In my analysis of reports from many people with autism, it appears that the faulty manner in which their brains process incoming information can be grouped into three basic categories: 1) sensory oversensitivity; 2) perceptual problems; and 3) difficulties organizing information.

Sensory Oversensitivity

From child to child, sensory oversensitivity is very variable. It can range from mild (slight anxiety when the environment is too loud, too bright, or too chaotic) to severe, with an individual going into a screaming tantrum every time he is in a large supermarket. One child may not tolerate fluorescent lights; another, like me, fears sudden loud noise because it hurts his ears. Children may be gagged by certain smells such as perfumes. The taste and/or texture of foods can be repulsive. Light touch can be merely annoying or actually painful. One child may enjoy water play and splashing and another may run screaming from it. Some individuals on the spectrum are attracted to objects that move rapidly and others will avoid them. When senses are disordered, the attention and concentration that learning requires becomes difficult and in some cases, impossible. Children who spend their days fearful of people and places that, through past experience, have been overwhelming to their senses, have little chance to relax enough to take notice of the learning opportunities being presented.

Perceptual Problems

Problems in this category often determine the style of learning that will be most effective. A child with poor auditory perception may hear sound like a bad mobile phone connection, where the voice fades in and out or entire parts of the communication are missing. The child is more likely to learn best with visually presented information. A child with visual perception problems may learn best through the auditory channel. Children who look out the corner of their eye while reading often have visual processing problems. Suspect a visual processing problem in children who finger-flick in front of their eyes, or hate either fluorescent lights or escalators. To some of these individuals, the world looks like it is viewed through a kaleidoscope: flat, without depth perception, and broken into pieces. For others, it is like looking through a small tube, seeing only the small circle of vision directly in front of them, with no peripheral vision. Some nonverbal individuals have both visual and auditory processing problems. They may learn best through their sense of touch and smell. For instance, to learn to get ready in the morning, they may need to be "walked" through (hand-over-hand) tasks such as putting on socks or pouring cereal. They may learn letters and numbers best when they can touch them, and trace their shape with their hands or fingers. Representative objects rather than visual charts can be useful in helping these individuals know when it is time to transition to a new activity.

Organizing Information

Because of these faulty connections in the brain, an individual may receive information but be unable to organize it or make sense of it. Donna Williams, a well-known person with autism from Australia, mentions that speech sounds like "blah-blah-blah" and the meaning disappears. She is hearing the words clearly but not understanding them. Problems with organizing information affect children's ability to form categories—the foundation for later concept formation. Difficulties people on the spectrum have with multi-tasking would also fall into this category. Again, these difficulties are highly variable, and range from mild to severe depending on which brain circuits connected and which ones did not during development. One classic test of flexible thinking is the Wisconsin Card Sorting Test. In this test, a person has to sort differently-patterned cards, one at a time, into categories such as *yellow* or *circles*. A person on the spectrum is slower to figure out new categories as they are introduced.

Sensory overload can cause either vision or hearing to shut down completely. During these times, no information will get through to the brain, and learning will not occur. Also, sensory and information processing problems are worse when a child is tired. It is therefore best to teach difficult material when the child is alert and wide awake. Since my oversensitivity to noise was fairly mild, I responded well to a gently intrusive teaching method where the teacher grabbed my chin to make me pay attention. Donna Williams told me that method absolutely would not work with her. The tactile input coupled with the teacher speaking would be overload and could not be processed simultaneously. Donna is a mono-channel learner. She either has to look at something or listen to something, but she cannot look and listen at the same time. Information processing on more than one sensory channel is not possible.

An effective teacher with spectrum children and adults is one who is a good detective and looks for the source of learning difficulties.

Often they can be found in one or a combination of these categories mentioned above. A challenge, even one considered mild, will dramatically compromise a child's ability to learn via traditional teaching methods. Teachers who truly want to help students with sensory and perception difficulties will figure out the child's unique learning style and adapt teaching methods accordingly. Some children do best with written instructions and assignments; others will do best through oral methods or oral testing. The best teachers have a flexible approach and teach to the style through which each child learns.

REFERENCE

Gastgeb, H.Z., M.S. Strauss, and N.J. Minshew. 2006. Do individuals with autism process categories differently? The effect of typicality and development. *Child Development* 77: 1717-1729.

Understanding Nonverbal Autism

Chapter

4

You Asked Me!
Tito Lives in a World of Sensory Scrambling
Solving Behavior Problems in Nonverbal Individuals with Autism
Whole-Task Teaching for Individuals with Severe Autism

These individuals are highly
aware of their surroundings
and have self-learned far more
than parents and teachers imagine.
It's their bodies that don't work,
not their minds.

TO UNDERSTAND THE MIND OF A CHILD OR ADULT WHO IS COMpletely nonverbal, without oral, sign, or written language, you must leave the world of thinking in words. This can be quite challenging for many people. Our society functions through the spoken word. For the majority of people, words are their "native language." It is difficult for them to step outside this very basic way of relating and imagine something else. Some neurotypicals, especially those with stronger creative sides, can do this. Other neurotypicals struggle immensely in understanding this concept.

I think in pictures; it's been that way forever for me. When I was very young, before any speech/language training, there were no words in my head. Now, words narrate the pictures in my imagination, but pictures remain my primary "language."

For a minute, try to imagine a land of picture-based or sensory-based thoughts. The closest analogy that may make sense to the neurotypical who thinks in words is to recall a recent dream. Many dreams do not contain language. They are a flowing sequence of pictures with associated emotional impressions. Sometimes these pictorial narrations make sense and we come away with a "message" from the dream. Many times, however, the images are strange, disconnected with one another, and we awake, scratching our heads and wondering "What was *that* dream all about?"

To imagine a nonverbal person's world, I shut my eyes and think with each of my individual senses. What would thinking in touch be like? How might I function if I could only relate to my world through my sense of smell? As an exercise in touch and smell thought, the reader could think about a vacation on the beach. There are usually vivid impressions of the color and sound of the ocean, the feel of the warm sand, etc. When a nonverbal person thinks or daydreams, there are no words going through his head. There are only sensory impressions such as images, sounds, smells, touch, and taste sensations coming into his consciousness. If the person has severe problems with both visual and auditory processing, his brain may rely on his other senses to make sense of his world. His thoughts may be only in touch, taste, or smell sensations. These forms of data input may be the only way he obtains accurate information about his environment. This may explain why some nonverbal individuals touch, tap, and smell things. It's how they learn about their world.

Our typical way of life, and especially our education system, is largely based on visual and auditory sharing of information. Imagine how difficult mere existence would be if those information channels were constantly turned off or functioned poorly in an individual. Parents, teachers, and therapists need to be good detectives in working with nonverbal individuals to figure out which senses are working best. For some, the auditory sense is preferred and for others, it's vision. For a minority, the sense of touch may be the primary learning channel. A basic principle is to use the sensory system that works the best. However, this will be highly variable among different nonverbal individuals.

Nonverbal with Cognitive Impairment and Nonverbal Without

The reader may wonder where I concocted all these ideas about nonverbal people's perceptions. They are based on neuroscience knowledge coupled with reports from many verbal individuals who can describe their very severe sensory problems. Many individuals who have more severe sensory problems than mine describe sensory scrambling or the shutdown of one or more senses. This occurs more frequently when they are tired or in a highly stimulating environment such as a large supermarket. Included in this section is an article about Tito, a nonverbal individual who can type and, in striking detail, describe his inner world. He has written about disordered, jumbled visual perceptions. He has also described a thinking self that exists separate from an acting self. He cannot control some of his flapping movements. His mind and body are not integrated together.

As a society, we equate intelligence with language. Smart people are verbal people; verbal people who can express themselves better than most are assumed even more intelligent. People who can't use language well are perceived as dumb. We don't usually stop and question whether oral motor skills, rather than intelligence skills, might be causing the language impairment. No, we do just the opposite and almost instantaneously judge the nonverbal person as being mentally impaired. Poor kid/adult; he can't talk. And, in our minds we continue with the most damaging thought of all: *and therefore he has nothing to say.*

This is very true within the autism community. We assume those who are nonverbal—especially children who have been nonverbal since birth—have reduced or limited cognitive abilities. The DSM-IV (Diagnostic and Statistical Manual, 4th edition) definition of autism states that 75% of these individuals function at a mentally retarded level based on IQ scores. This sets up a vicious cycle: we expect less from these kids, so they receive fewer opportunities to learn. We don't challenge them to learn because we've already decided they can't. We test these children for IQ, using testing instruments that are largely ill-suited to this population, and then point to their low scores as confirmations of impaired mental functioning.

The way I see it, it's time we rethink nonverbal individuals with autism and realize that the preconceived notions under which we've been relating to and educating this population over the last twenty years may be flat-out wrong. Luckily, other professionals in the autism community are coming to the same conclusion, and research is shedding light on the hidden abilities within this population. Professionals have generally agreed that about 50% of individuals with autism will never speak. Catherine Lord, a University of Michigan pioneer in autism research, is suggesting we may be way off the mark. In her 2004 study sample of children diagnosed and treated at age two, only 14% remained nonverbal by age nine, and 35-45% could speak fluently.

Our current perceptions about nonverbal individuals with autism are also being stretched by people on the spectrum, like Tito and others, who are coming forth and writing about their rich inner worlds, their abilities, and bit by bit, deflating the notion that not being able to speak means having nothing to say. Through the increased use of augmentative and alternative communication aids with nonverbal individuals, we are discovering that many children with autism have taught themselves to read, some in more than one language; that these individuals are highly aware of their surroundings and have self-learned far more than parents and teachers imagine. It's their bodies that don't work, not their minds.

And these individuals have a lot to say. Amanda Baggs is one such woman, and her nine-minute YouTube clip, "In My Language," is illuminating to all who watch it. As it opens we see her rocking back and forth, flapping her hands in front of a large window. She goes through a series of odd repetitive behaviors, all the while accompanied by an almost eerie hum: swatting at a necklace with her hand, slapping a sheet of paper against a window, running her hand over a computer keyboard, flicking a metal band against a door knob. Then the words "A Translation" appear on the screen, and the 27-year-old nonverbal autistic mesmerizes us with a highly articulate explanation of her thoughts and her actions. She explains how touch, taste, and smell provide her with a "constant conversation" with her environment. She challenges our neurotypical way of thinking about nonverbal individuals in a manner that cannot be ignored. And I, for one, applaud her and others who are speaking out about what it means, and doesn't mean, to be nonverbal people with autism. It's about time.

In our interactions with nonverbal individuals with autism, it is critical that we accurately determine their level of ability and challenge, and not automatically make assumptions based on their verbal language capabilities, nor their IQ scores. It is true that many highly impaired individuals with autism exist who also have accompanying mental retardation. But that percentage may be far less than what we currently assume.

Slow Processing of Information

For most nonverbal and impaired individuals with ASD, the brain processes information very slowly. They may have fewer input channels open to receive information, or their connections may work like dial-up rather than high-speed internet connections. They need much more time to switch gears between different tasks. In autism and many other developmental disorders, attention-shifting is slow, and nonverbal impaired individuals are often slower than individuals with milder forms of autism. In her lectures, Lorna King, one of the early pioneers in using sensory integration, warned all therapists attending her meetings about a phenomenon called "clipping." Clipping can occur in individuals who are both verbal and nonverbal. Attention-shifting can be so slow that the person may miss half the information the teacher is trying to convey to them. This is most likely to happen when the child's attention has to be shifted to a new task. For example, if I said to a child playing with his toy "The juice is on the table" the child may hear only "on the table." To avoid this problem, the parent or teacher should first capture the child's attention with a phrase like, "Tommy, I need to tell you something." Then deliver the instruction or important information. If half of the first phrase is "clipped" it does not matter, because now the input channel is open and the statement about the juice can get through.

Fear is the Main Emotion

All behavior occurs for a reason. When a nonverbal impaired person has a tantrum, fear may be the main motivator. In my own case, little high-pitched noises that occur at night still set off a little twinge of fear in me. The heart-pounding big fear reactions I used to have during my twenties are now controlled with anti-depressant drugs. Trying to eliminate these big fear reactions through cognitive or behavioral methods didn't work for me. Self-reports from other individuals also indicate that certain sounds or sensations cause panic attacks. If an individual is nonverbal and their receptive learning is impaired, harmless things such as a certain room or a particular person may be associated with a stimulus that hurts, such as a smoke alarm. In some cases, the individual might associate the dreadful sound with something he was looking at when the alarm went off. If he was looking at a teacher's blue jacket, he may develop a blue jacket fear. I know this sounds odd, but these associative fear memories occur all the time in animals. A dog often fears the place where he got hit by a car instead of being afraid of cars. If these associations can be figured out, it may be possible to remove the feared object. I discuss fear memories in more depth in my book, *Animals in Translation*.

An individual with severe autism can easily panic if something new is suddenly introduced. A surprise birthday party can trigger a tantrum instead of pleasure. It is best to gradually habituate the child to the things he or she will experience at the party. This is very similar to habituating horses to tolerate the new scary things they will see at a horse show. They need to gradually get used to new things such as flags and balloons at home before they go to a show. Individuals with severe autism can learn to like new things. The best way to introduce them is to let the child or adult gradually approach and explore them at their own pace and inclination. Some nonverbal individuals may explore them by touching, smelling, or tasting. They need to be provided with a specific place where they are allowed to do this kind of exploration, because licking things at the grocery store is not appropriate behavior. Nonverbal impaired people are usually able to learn that certain activities are only allowed in certain places. For instance, if the person does not want to taste a new food, he may need to explore it first by touching it. This activity should be done away from the dining room because touching and smearing food is not appropriate behavior in the dining room.

Self-Injurious Behavior (SIB)

Some nonverbal individuals, and even some highly verbal individuals, engage in banging their heads or biting themselves. Reports from people on the spectrum have revealed that many of these problems stem from severe sensory issues. In this case, the child may be hypo-sensitive—lacking in sensory input—rather than the more typical hypersensitivity (too much input) that is often the case within the autism population. In some of these cases, individuals do not realize they are being self-injurious because they have tactile or body boundary issues. For example, when they are tired or upset they cannot determine where their foot ends and the floor begins. They may not feel themselves sitting on a chair at school, so they squirm or bounce in the chair to induce the sensory input they need to feel stable. Lorna King found that a child who self abuses often feels no pain. Children may dig at their skin to the point of drawing blood because their sensory receptors return them no tactile sensation as they would in a typical person. After King introduced children to activities that provided calming sensory stimulation, such as deep pressure or slow swinging, pain sensation returned. She has seen children who used to head bang start to hit their heads and stop before they did so because they know it will hurt now.

The best approach for controlling SIB is an integrated approach. A combination of behavioral analysis, sensory therapy, conventional medications, and biomedical interventions such as diets and supplements often works best. The big mistake that many people make on treating SIB is to get too single-minded in their approach. Some people try to use just behavioral analysis and never use a drug. Others use drugs and nothing else. Both single-minded approaches are wrong. A drug-only approach leads to a sleepy "drug zombie" and a behavior-only approach without any intervention to reduce nervous system arousal may lead to bad procedures, such as long periods of restraint.

Does the Nonverbal Person Understand Speech?

In some cases, a nonverbal person has receptive language and can understand what is being said; in other cases, they do not. Nonverbal people are masters at reading slight differences in a teacher's or parent's actions. I had one parent tell me their child has ESP because he is already waiting at the door *before* his mother even gets her car keys or purse. It is likely that the individual is sensing slight differences in behavior before it's time to get the keys or purse. There may be some hustle and bustle activities such as throwing out the newspaper. If the child has severe visual processing problems, he may be responding to the sound of the paper being crushed in the trash can.

In some situations, the nonverbal individual may be responding to a gesture rather than a word. If you point to the juice or turn your head towards it, the person may perceive your actions. One way to test receptive language is to ask the person to do something odd. An example would be ask the child to put his book on the chair. In some nonverbal individuals, verbal language is impossible, but they learn to read and express themselves through typing. Their speech circuits are scrambled but they can still communicate through the typed word.

ADDITIONAL READING

Fouse, B., and M. Wheeler. 1997. *A treasure chest of behavioral strategies for individuals with autism.* Arlington, Texas: Future Horizons, Inc.

Grandin, T., and C. Johnson. 2005. *Animals in translation.* New York: Scribner.

Horvath, K., and J.A. Perman. 2002. Autism and gastrointestinal symptoms. *Current Gastroenterology Reports* 4: 251-258.

Kern, J.K. et al. 2007. Sensory correlations in autism. *Autism* 11: 123-134.

Muchopadhyay, T.J. 2004. *The mind tree*. New York: Arcade Publishing.

Savarese, R.J. 2007. *Reasonable people: A memoir of autism and adoption: On the meaning of family and the politics of neurological difference*. New York: Other Press. (It describes successful teaching strategies for teaching nonverbal people to type.)

Schaller, S. 1995. *A man without words*. Berkeley, CA: University of California Press.

Williams, D. 1996. *Autism—An Inside-Out Approach*. London, England: Jessica Kingsley Publishers.

Wolfgang, A., Pierce L. Teder-Salejarvi, E. Courchesne, and S.A. Hillyard. 2005. Auditory spatial localization and attention deficits in autistic adults. *Cognitive Brain Research* 23: 221-234.

Wolman, D. 2008. The truth about autism: Scientists reconsider what they think they know. *Wired Magazine* 16.03.

A good teacher has good instincts
and knows how much a child
has to be pushed to get progress.

You Asked Me!

PARENTS AND TEACHERS FREQUENTLY ASK ME QUESTIONS ABOUT THEIR child or the student(s) with whom they work. To follow are a few of the questions I have been asked repeatedly. I hope they prove informative and useful to your own situation.

—TEMPLE

Q: My nine-year-old son is well-behaved when he is with me (his mom) but screams, kicks, and tears his books at school. What causes this?

A: When I was nine, maintaining a consistent environment at both home and school prevented this problem. I knew that if I misbehaved at school there would be consequences when I got home. A tantrum at school always resulted in loss of watching TV for one night (taking it away for a month would seem like five years to a nine-year-old). When I got home, mother would calmly tell me that Mrs. Dietch had called, so no TV. I knew what the rule was.

There are a lot of possible reasons for behavior problems at school. The foremost cause that needs to be ruled out (or addressed!) is over-stimulation from fluorescent lights, and noises, such as the school bell. Loud noises hurt the ears of many children with autism. A child may have a tantrum in the classroom because he never knows when the dreaded fire alarm might go off. If sensory problems are not a part of the behavior problem, it may be that the child is testing you (like most nine-year-olds will); adhering to prescribed rules is more important than ever if this is the case. Last, not every child enjoys school; the child may simply not want to be there. Again, consistent actions and expectations on your part will help immensely. It is important to make sure you tell your son what the rules are and what behaviors you expect of him.

Q: Do rituals and stereotypies differ from obsessive-compulsive behavior?

A: There are several different motivations for the repetitive behavior in children with autism. I needed to dribble sand through my hands to screen out loud sounds that hurt my ears. I would tune out the world. Fortunately, my teachers did not allow me to tune the world out. A second motivation for repetitive behaviors is sudden sensory overload. For instance, a child may suddenly flap his arms when he enters a large supermarket. A third motivation is a neurological tic. This is most likely to occur in nonverbal adults. In some cases the person has little or no voluntary control over the movement.

Obsessive compulsive behavior (OCD) is repetitive behavior that occurs on a less primitive level. In non-autistic adults, OCD often manifests itself as washing one's hands over and over or constantly checking to see if the doors are locked. Some researchers believe that OCD is caused by a malfunction in the brain circuits that motivate hygiene and checking for danger. These are old, primitive circuits that humans share with animals.

Another repetitive behavior is perseveration. I used to ask the same question over and over. I asked my grandfather a hundred times "Why is the sky blue?" I enjoyed hearing his answer. Perseveration and OCD are probably related. Both behaviors are often alleviated by medications such as Prozac. When I took antidepressants when I was 31, my tendency to perseverate on one topic was greatly reduced. In me, antidepressants reduced anxiety. Reducing anxiety helped to reduce perseveration. From a social perspective, I also had to learn that other people were bored when I discussed the same topics over and over.

Q: How does a teacher know how much to "push" a child to get progress?

A: A good teacher has good instincts and knows how much a child has to be pushed to get progress. Part of this skill comes through keen observation and paying close attention to both the child's interior and exterior world. My speech teacher would grab my chin to make me pay attention. She could kind of yank me out of my autistic world. If she pushed too hard I had a tantrum and if she did not push enough, I made no progress. She had to be "gently insistent." I was a child with relatively mild sensory processing problems. I responded well to a "get in my face" method.

A child with more severe sensory processing problems may go into sensory shut down if a teacher grabs his chin. The child will make more progress if the teacher talks quietly. Children's learning styles vary widely, especially children on the autism spectrum. For one type of child the teacher can "yank open their front door"; for the other type of child, the teacher must "sneak quietly in their back door."

When I asked him what his life
was like before he learned to type,
he responded with the word "empty."

✫

Tito Lives in a World
of Sensory Scrambling

I N A PREVIOUS ARTICLE, I DISCUSSED THE IMPORTANCE OF INCORPO-
rating sensory integration into the treatment program for a person
with ASD. In this article, a real-life example illustrates how far-reach-
ing can be the impact of sensory impairment in a child's life.

I first met Tito Mukhopadhyay* in a quiet medical library. He
looked like a typical nonverbal, low-functioning teenager with autism.
When he entered the room, he picked up a bright yellow journal and
smelled it. He then ran around and flapped. His mother pulled him
over to the computer where I sat and invited me to ask Tito a question
about autism. I told her I wanted to ask him about something different, where cueing or prior memorization of an answer would be
impossible. From the bottom of a nearby pile of magazines I found an
old *Scientific American*. As I thumbed through the magazine I found
an illustration of an astronaut riding a horse. When I showed Tito the
picture he quickly typed "Apollo II on a horse." This convinced me
there was a good brain trapped inside Tito's dysfunctional body.

At a recent conference in Canada, I had another opportunity to talk
with Tito. Throughout our conversation, his mother had to keep
prompting him to attend to the computer and respond to my questions. I was curious about his sensory systems, so I asked him what his
vision was like. He said he saw fragments of color, shapes, and motion.
This is a more severe version of the fragmented perception that Donna

Williams has described in her books. When I asked him what his life was like before he learned to type, he responded with the word "empty." Despite intervention, Tito still has a very short attention span. He could type only a few short sentences while we were together before he succumbed to sensory overload.

Visual processing challenges such as Tito experiences may stem from abnormal brain connections, according to Dr. Eric Courchesne. The brain has three types of visual perception circuits, each different for color, shape, and motion. In the typical brain, these circuits work together to merge the three visual components into a stable image. Research has shown that in autism there is a lack of interconnections between different parts of the brain. Dr. Eric Courchesne suggests that in autistic brains, large neurons that integrate different brain systems together are abnormal. He states autism may be an unusual disconnection disorder.

Not all nonverbal children with autism can be like Tito, but he is a prime example of a person with a part of the brain having many broken connections with the outside world. Because of their fragmented abilities, it is important that parents and professionals introduce different modes of communication and social connection, like the keyboard, to children with ASD at an early age so that another Tito is not trapped in emptiness.

* At the age of three, Tito Mukhopadhyay was diagnosed with severe autism, but his mother, Soma, refused to accept the conventional wisdom of the time that her son would be unable to interact with the outside world. She read to him, taught him to write in English, and challenged him to write his own stories. The result of their efforts is a remarkable book, *The Mind Tree: A Miraculous Child Breaks the Silence of Autism*, written when Tito was between eight and eleven years old. It comprises a broad collection of profound and startling philosophical writings about growing up under the most challenging of circumstances, and how it feels to be locked inside an autistic body and mind.

REFERENCE

Courchesne, E. 2004. Brain development in autism: Early overgrowth followed by premature arrest of growth. *Mental Retardation and Developmental Disabilities* 10: 106-111.

If a functional communication
system has not been put
into place with a child,
his only recourse is behavior.

Solving Behavior Problems in Nonverbal Individuals with Autism

B EHAVIOR PROBLEMS IN NONVERBAL INDIVIDUALS WITH AUTISM ARE often difficult to alleviate because these people cannot tell you how they feel. However, all behavior is communication. As a parent, educator, or caregiver, you have to learn to be a good detective to figure out why a nonverbal person with autism is acting out.

If a nonverbal individual who is generally calm suddenly becomes aggressive or frequent tantrums arise, first look for a hidden painful medical problem. Some of the common sources are ear infections, a bad toothache, a sinus infection, gastro-intestinal problems, acid reflex (heartburn), and constipation. You need to be observant; the individual may touch or clutch at the area of the body that hurts, avoid certain foods they previously enjoyed, or their sleep patterns may be different.

Sensory overload is a second—and more frequent—cause of behavior outbursts. A tantrum in Wal-Mart or other such crowded stores is usually due to sensory overstimulation. Behavior tantrums at school may arise during or prior to times when many students are gathered together, such as recess, lunchtime, or assemblies. Stimuli that are most likely to cause problems are the flicker of fluorescent lights, perfumes/colognes and other strong smells (the cafeteria at school, the store's bakery or seafood section, the restaurant's kitchen), and high-pitched sounds such as squeaky wheels on shopping carts, store product announcements, or smoke alarms. An individual who had previously been calm or cooperative may be afraid to go into a store or a room where a microphone once had audio feedback and squealed. A place that he previously liked may now be too scary because of the association with noxious stimuli. Sounds, smells, and textures that are merely annoying to typical people may be like a dentist's drill hitting a nerve for a person with autism. I have difficulty tolerating scratchy clothes, but for some more sensitive individuals, scratchy sweaters, stiff new clothes, or double-stitched seams may cause a pain sensation. Often something as simple as changing to a new brand of socks may feel like walking on burning sandpaper.

If hidden medical problems and sensory issues are ruled out, the tantrums or outbursts may stem from a purely behavioral reason. The three major behavioral sources of tantrums, hitting and meltdowns are:

- frustration because the person cannot communicate
- the need for attention
- to escape from a task they do not want to do

Deciphering the correct motivator is important. Once the motivator has been found, a solution can be developed. Otherwise, while is it possible to extinguish an inappropriate behavior, in all likelihood an equally inappropriate behavior that meets the same need will develop. For example, ignoring the behavior is the correct response if the behavior motivator is to seek attention. However, this response would be the worst thing to do if the individual was frustrated because he could not communicate his need for help. Solutions to the behavior could include teaching the child sign language or to use an augmentative communication device. Or teaching the individual socially appropriate ways of saying "no" or expressing his desires.

Keeping a detailed diary will help you figure out the behavior motivation. One nonverbal boy screamed to get his mother to stop at

McDonald's because he had learned that it worked. However, he never screamed when his father was driving because he knew dad would not stop.

Frustration with not being able to communicate is a very common problem in nonverbal individuals with ASD; they *must* have a way to express their needs and wants. If a functional communication system has not been put into place with a child, his only recourse is behavior. I can remember screaming when I did not want to wear a hat. I had no other way to express my dislike for it, nor to communicate that for me, the hat was disturbing on a sensory level.

Consistency is calming; surprises produce anxiety in most individuals with ASD. They need to know what is coming up next. Sensory processing systems in some of these individuals are so disordered that touch and smell are the only two senses that provide reliable, accurate information to the person's brain. If their visual and auditory systems are giving them jumbled information, they may rely more on touch. This is why some nonverbal people tap things like a blind person navigating with a cane. The neurological feedback this provides is calming to their senses. It also explains some of the repetitive behaviors common to individuals with autism. The consistency provided by doing the same thing again and again—and getting the same result—alleviates some of the anxiety associated with the rest of the world being in a constant state of change.

Because of the visual processing problems experienced by many nonverbal individuals with ASD, picture schedules may work poorly with some of them. At one group home, many outbursts and tantrums were avoided by using a touch schedule instead of a picture schedule. Ten minutes before breakfast, they were given a spoon to hold and ten minutes before a shower, they were given a wash cloth. The tangible object communicated what was to happen and the ten-minute period gave their brains time to process the sensory information.

Research is also now showing very clearly that exercise will reduce anxiety and stereotypical behavior. At another group home, a program of vigorous exercise reduced behavior problems.

Some nonverbal teenagers and adults on the spectrum may need medication to alleviate stress and anxiety so that other forms of behavior modification can be used successfully. Often a combination of approaches is best. Sometimes a small dose of conventional medication combined with dietary or other biomedical treatment is more effective than either method used alone.

REFERENCES

Coleman, R.S. et al. 1976. The effects of fluorescent and incandescent illumination upon repetitive behaviors in autistic children. *Journal of Autism and Developmental Disorders* 6: 157-162.

Strohle, A. et al. 2005. The acute antipanic activity of exercise. *American Journal of Psychiatry* 162: 2376-2378.

Walters, R.G. and W.E. Walters. 1980. Decreasing self-stimulatory behaviors with physical exercise in a group of autistic boys. *Journal of Autism and Developmental Disorders* 10: 379-387.

Whole-Task Teaching
for Individuals
with Severe Autism

THE STANDARD METHOD FOR TEACHING A NONVERBAL PERSON with autism tasks such as dressing or cooking is to provide a picture schedule that shows the steps of the task. This works well for many individuals, but some have difficulty linking the steps together. To learn a simple task such as making a sandwich, they have to see a person demonstrate the **entire** task, from start to finish, with no steps left out. If they do not see how the second slice of bread gets on top of the peanut butter they may not try to perform the individual steps because, as a whole, they do not make sense to the individual. Sandwich-making is easy to teach because when the task is demonstrated, the **entire** task is observed, and the end product—the sandwich—is concrete and has meaning to the individual.

This idea of "whole-task teaching" is particularly relevant in the area of toilet training. One of the challenges with toilet training individuals on the severe end of the spectrum is that the individual may not know how the urine or feces gets into the toilet. The picture schedule shows the waste in the toilet, but it does not show how it got there. There are often more problems with teaching the person to defecate in the toilet compared to urination. This is because the individual has more likely been able to directly observe how urine comes out of the person and goes into the toilet. This is especially true with boys, but even girls can observe this. It is not as obvious an action—for either sex—when it comes to defecating. If seeing how the waste goes from the person to the toilet is left out of the teaching sequence, these individuals may not know what they have to do.

Furthermore, neurotypicals assume a picture is all that's needed to help the child or adult link the elimination of bodily waste to the place where it should go, i.e., the toilet. But for many individuals that link is too broad a jump and does not "compute" in their brain. Those with severe sensory issues may not feel the sensation of having to urinate or understand how to bear down to defecate. These are intermittent steps that may need to be addressed for a successful toileting program.

Sometimes even demonstrating a whole task via visual teaching is not enough. Many individuals on the severe end of the spectrum have so many visual processing problems that they have to learn tasks by touch. One therapist taught a child how to use a playground slide by "walking" him through the entire task hand-over-hand with no steps left out. To understand how to climb the ladder and go down the slide, the therapist stood behind the child and moved his hands and feet through the entire sequence: climbing the ladder, sitting on the slide, and going down it.

Teaching how a foot is put into a shoe can be done in a similar manner. The therapist, hand-over-hand, guides the individual's hand over the ankle and foot so the person can feel the foot, then feel the inside of the shoe so they can cognitively link how the foot could slide into the shoe. The next step, hand-over-hand, is to slip the foot into the shoe in one continuous motion, so the individual experiences the feeling of the foot going into the shoe and makes the cognitive connection through the tactile information being received.

Individuals on the more severe end of the autism spectrum can be taught to perform different actions, but we must not lose sight of the accompanying sensory issues that can impede their learning. In many cases, these sensory issues are severe and rob the individual of much of the "data feedback" necessary for learning that neurotypicals receive unconsciously. Whole-task, visual, and tactile-based teaching strategies can supply the extra information these individuals need in order to learn.

Behavior
Issues

Chapter

5

Disability versus Just Bad Behaviors
My Experience with Teasing and Bullying
Rudeness is Inexcusable
Autism & Religion: Teach Goodness

Behavior never occurs in a vacuum;
it is the end result of the interaction
between the child and his or
her environment, and that
environment includes the people in it.

✵

B EHAVIOR IS ONE OF THE MOST WIDELY DISCUSSED TOPICS OF ALL
times by parents and professionals within the autism community.
Parents want to know how to deal with their child's behaviors at home
and in the community. Educators in the classroom find it difficult to
manage the behavior outbursts that can accompany autism, and often
resort to punitive tactics, which have little or no effect on an autistic
child who is having a tantrum due to sensory overload. Understanding
the source of "bad" behavior and teaching "good" behaviors is a challenge for neurotypical adults who have a different way of thinking and
sensing their world than do children with ASD. It requires adults to
rethink the way they interact with people with ASD, and most are ill-
equipped to do so. Abstract concepts about morality and behavior do
not work. The child has to learn by specific examples. When I said
something rude about the appearance of a lady at a store, mother
instantly corrected me and explained that commenting on how fat the
person is was rude. I had to learn the concept of "rude behavior" by
being corrected every time I did a rude behavior. Behavior has to be
taught one *specific* example at a time.

Call me old-fashioned, but adults in the world of my youth, the '50s
and '60s, believed in a stricter social behavior code than do adults in
today's world. For the child with ASD, that was a good thing. Social
skills were taught as a matter of course. Behavior rules were straightforward and strictly enforced, another positive strategy well aligned
with the autism way of thinking. Consequences were uniformly
imposed and expectations to behave were high. My mother and all the
other mothers who lived in our neighborhood attended to children's
behaviors, and placed value on teaching their children good manners
and appropriate behaviors. To be a functioning member of society,
these things were required, not optional, as they seem to be today. Kids

today are allowed to do just about anything. The behavior of many five- or six-year-olds I've witnessed in stores or other public places is atrocious. The parent stands there, not knowing what to do, eventually giving in to the child's tantrum just to get him quiet.

Today's fast paced, techno-driven world is louder and busier than the world I grew up in. That, in and of itself, creates new challenges for the child with autism, whose sensory systems are usually impaired in one way or another. Our senses are bombarded on a daily basis, and this can render even typical children and adults exhausted by the end of the day. Imagine the effect it has on the sensory-sensitive systems of the child with autism, especially those with hyper-acute senses. They enter the world with a set of physical challenges that severely impair their ability to tolerate life, let alone learn within conventional environments. They have so much farther to go to be ready to learn than I did growing up in my time.

When figuring out how to handle behavior problems, one has to ask: Is it a *sensory* problem or a *behavior* problem? Accommodations are usually needed to help a child handle problems with sensory over-sensitivity. Punishing sensory problems will just make the child's behavior *worse*. Sometimes behavior problems occur when an individual with ASD becomes frustrated due to slower mental processing, which in turn makes a quick response difficult. In kindergarten, I threw a huge tantrum because the teacher did not give me enough time to explain the mistakes I had made on an assignment. The task was to mark pictures of things that began with the letter B. I was marked wrong for marking a picture of a suitcase with the letter B. In our house, suitcases were called "bags."

Behavior never occurs in a vacuum; it is the end result of the interaction between the child and his or her environment, and that environment includes the people in it. To bring about positive change in the behavior of the child with ASD, adults need to first adjust their own behaviors. Supernanny Jo Frost makes such remarkable changes in the behavior of kids because she first helps parents get control of their own behaviors and learn basic behavior techniques. That's a valuable lesson for every parent, educator, or service provider, to take to heart. The behavior, good or bad, of a child with ASD, largely depends on you and your behavior. If you want to change the behavior of the child, first look at your own. You might be surprised by what you see.

The way I see it, many parents
and teachers do not hold high
enough expectations for good behavior
from these individuals, nor do they hold
them responsible for their behaviors.

✬

Disability versus Just Bad Behaviors

DURING MY TRAVELS, I HAVE OBSERVED THAT MANY CHILDREN ON the autism spectrum need more discipline. Many parents and teachers seem confused about the cause of some of the behaviors that surface from within their kids. Is it just bad behavior or is the problem behavior caused by the person's disability?

Teachers and parents need to differentiate between a troublesome behavior caused by sensory problems and just plain bad behavior. This is especially true for highly verbal autistic and Asperger's children. The way I see it, many parents and teachers do not hold high enough expectations for good behavior from these individuals, nor do they hold them responsible for their behaviors. My being raised during the 1950s probably was an advantage. Life was much more structured then. I was expected to behave when my family sat down for dinner. It was quiet at the house during dinner so there were no problems with sensory overload. Today, in the average household, dinner can be noisy, chaotic, and stressful for a child on the spectrum. Music is playing or the TV is on, or siblings are all talking or yelling at one time. To my mother's credit, she was also a good detective about what environments caused me stress. She recognized that large, noisy crowds or too much noise and commotion in general was more than my nervous system could handle. When I had a tantrum, she understood why.

Bad behaviors should have consequences, and parents need to understand that applying consequences in a consistent manner will make gains in changing these behaviors. I behaved well at the dining room table because there were consequences: I lost TV privileges for one night if I misbehaved at the table. Other misbehaving, such as swearing or laughing at a fat lady, had consequences. Mother knew how to make consequences meaningful, too. She chose those things that were important to me as my lost privileges.

I was always testing the limits, as most children will. Parents should not think that because their child has autism or Asperger's this will not happen. Mother made sure there was consistent discipline at home, and between home and school. She, my nanny, and my teacher worked together. There was no way I could manipulate one against the other.

The table on the following page shows some examples of "just bad behavior" and some of the more common behavior problems caused by either high-functioning autism or Asperger's Syndrome. Many of these examples came directly from parents and teachers I've met at workshops and conferences. Bad behavior needs discipline. But parents must never punish a child with autism for acting out, or having a tantrum, when it is caused by sensory overload or some other part of autism, such as not comprehending what is expected of him or her, or never being taught appropriate social skills. If you know your child well, and understand how the various sensory and social systems are affected by autism, you'll know when your child's behavior is "just plain bad" and when it's a manifestation of his or her autism.

BAD BEHAVIOR that should be corrected
Autism or Asperger's Syndrome is NOT an excuse

- Sloppy table manners
- Dressing like a slob; poor grooming
- Being rude to either a teacher, a parent, another adult, or a peer
- Swearing
- Laughing inappropriately at people (e.g., at a fat lady, someone in a wheelchair)
- Inappropriate sexual behavior in public
- Manipulating adults by throwing fits at home, school or in the community
- Stealing a toy and then lying about it
- Cheating at a card game or during a sports activity

✹

Behavior Problems caused by Autism or Asperger's Syndrome
ACCOMMODATIONS may be required

- Screaming when the fire alarm rings because it hurts his ears
- Tantruming in a large, busy supermarket/mall/recreation area due to sensory overload; more likely to occur when the child is tired
- Removing clothes/excessive scratching/itching: cannot tolerate feel of certain fabrics, seams, fibers against skin
- Hyperactivity and agitation under fluorescent lighting
- Sloppy handwriting: often due to poor fine-motor skills. (Allow child to use typewriter or computer instead.)

"Sticks and stones will
break your bones but words
will never hurt you."
It's not true; words hurt a lot.

✦

My Experience with Teasing and Bullying

I N ELEMENTARY SCHOOL, I HAD FRIENDS BECAUSE THE OTHER CHIL-
dren enjoyed doing craft projects with me. I was good at making
things that the other children were interested in, projects such as kites
or tree houses. My big problems happened in high school.

In high school, teenagers become purely social beings. Being good
at crafts or science projects did not score any points in the social scene.
The children's rhyme says, "Sticks and stones will break your bones but
words will never hurt you." It's not true; words hurt a lot.

At first, my response to teasing was anger. I got kicked out of a large
girls' school for throwing a book at a girl who called me a "retard." In
ninth grade, I went to a small boarding school for gifted but troubled
students. Within the first week, the teasing started. They called me
"bones" because I was skinny, and "tape recorder." I responded with
fists. After a major fistfight in the cafeteria, I had horseback riding
privileges revoked. Since I really wanted to ride the horses, I stopped
fighting. The consequence for fist fighting had an impact on me.

However, the strong emotions I felt did not just go away. I had to
find an outlet for the emotion—it could not just be shut off. So I
started crying when I was teased. I wonder if some of the terrible problems with school shootings would stop if boys could react with tears
rather than anger. Teasing has been a major factor in many school

shootings. In our society, I think there is too much emphasis on teaching men to be tough.

Even today I defuse anger by crying. Angry outbursts would not be tolerated at work, but if I have to cry, I can find a private place.

When I went off to college at Franklin Pierce in New Hampshire, there were many good teachers who helped me. However, teasing was still a problem. They called me "buzzard woman." The turning point came—and the teasing stopped—when the other students found out that I had talents and useful skills that interested them. I became involved in the school talent show, working many hours making scenery, and acting in some of the skits. I made a sign for the Old Palace Theatre, covered with silver glitter, with orange and green lettering. I also sang some funny songs in a screeching voice.

Until a person participates in activities that are *shared* with other people, the teasing will continue. I strongly recommend that students with autism/AS get involved in special interest clubs in some of the areas they naturally excel at, activities such as computers, art, math, karate, etc. These clubs will help provide a refuge from teasing and improve the person's self-esteem. Socializing is easier, because he or she is with other people with similar interests.

As I have said many times before, talents need to be developed. Parents and teachers need to work on expanding the child's range of interests into areas that can be shared with other students. For example, the AS or autistic student may have good art skills, but all he draws are doorknobs. Skills such as drawing need to be broadened. A good first step may be to enroll the student in an art class where drawing other subjects is required. I can remember when I took a pencil sketching class and had to spend the entire two-hour class drawing my own shoe. At college, the other students didn't become interested in my artistic talents until I made scenery for the school show. We all shared a common goal—the show—and I became part of their "group."

While I made scenery for some of my high school plays, the young teenagers were too socially hyper to appreciate my abilities. Some gifted autistic or Asperger's students may need to be removed from this hyper-social high school scene. Enroll them in a university or community college course where they can be with their intellectual peers. College students are a bit more mature and they recognize and appreciate talents and don't tease as much. In high school, I dropped out of the teenage social scene because it was too hard for me to deal with. It was not until the college talent show that I was able to participate again.

The anger and resentment many
people with AS feel is understandable
and justified. What is not, however,
is rude "acting-out behavior"
in response to these feelings.

✦

Rudeness
is Inexcusable

RECENTLY I WENT TO A LARGE AUTISM MEETING HERE IN THE U.S. and was appalled at the rude behavior exhibited by a few adult individuals with Asperger's Syndrome (AS) who were also attending. One of them walked up to me and said, "Who the f—- are you?" He also interrupted two major sessions at the conference because he adamantly opposed the notion of finding a cure for autism. Later that day, this same individual ran a panel discussion where individuals with AS talked about their lives. During this session, his manners and behavior were polite and perfect, demonstrating he was capable of behaving properly when he wanted to.

What was most distressing to me was that these individuals felt that because they had Asperger's, the people around them should accept their rude behavior—that their "disability" made them somehow exempt from the social standards we all live by. Like it or not, social boundaries exist that we are expected to conform to, whether we're members of a "minority" population or mainstream American society. To be members of a group, we must all learn the rules and act in socially appropriate ways. People with autism and AS may find this more difficult to do, but being on the spectrum is not an exemption from doing so.

I wasn't entirely opposed to some of the viewpoints these individuals with AS shared with other conference attendees, but I couldn't help but think how much more effective they could have been in the delivery of their message so that other people at the conference would be willing to listen and consider what they had to say. Rude behavior has consequences, and in most cases, they are negative. In general, rude or overt anti-social behavior:

- is an instant turn-off to people; most people dislike people who are rude.

- makes people uncomfortable, uneasy.

- closes down channels of communication.

- results in people forming quick negative opinions about you, whether or not they are valid or based on fact.

- alienates you from others; it reduces the chance of further contact.

- is seen as individual weakness, as an inability of a person to be "in control" of his or her emotions.

Those of us with autism/AS live in a society that can be grossly ignorant of our needs, of the day-by-day difficulty we face in trying to "fit" into a world that is often harsh, stressful, and grating on our neurology. The anger and resentment many people with AS feel is understandable and justified. What is not, however, is rude "acting-out behavior" in response to these feelings, and calling that behavior acceptable in the name of autism.

The autism and the neurotypical cultures remain divided, yet that gap is slowly closing through education, awareness, and experiences. It happens one person at a time, and we each play a role in how quickly we close the gap. When individuals with AS tout a rigid belief that they should be allowed to act in any way they choose, exempt from the social rules that call for respect for our fellow man, they widen the chasm that still exists. It perpetuates a we-versus-them mentality: "You are wrong; we are right." It also perpetuates the very negative stereotypes some of us on the spectrum work to overturn: that people with AS are stubborn, resistant to change, and unwilling to compromise. While these may be characteristics of autism spectrum disorders, to put forth the notion that these are immutable, unchangeable personality traits only further supports the "inability" of people on the spectrum.

Teach your child love and
kindness in a concrete manner,
with very specific examples.

✶

Autism & Religion: Teach Goodness

MANY PARENTS SHARE WITH ME THEIR DESIRE TO EDUCATE THEIR child with autism or Asperger's about the religion practiced by the rest of their family. Some wonder if their child is capable of understanding the concept of God, or a higher power, of being spiritual, or even understanding the basic messages of the Bible or other religious texts.

I have learned, over the years, that there is a whole upper layer of abstract thought mixed with emotion that I do not have. Thoughts and emotions are separated in my mind; they don't intermingle and affect one another. Thinking is concrete—it happens in pictures in my mind. Therefore, for me, inspirational matters had no meaning, except for the very concrete aspects of them taught to me.

I had a proper religious upbringing, though. My family attended the Episcopalian church every Sunday. These weekly outings held little value to me, and I was not interested in what went on. Scratchy petticoats I had to wear to church were awful; in fact, the worst thing about church was the Sunday-best clothes. Sunday school was boring to me and I usually spent the entire class filling in the Os and Ps in the church program.

Concrete teachings were what I understood. For instance, our Christmas service made a lasting impression on me that I carry to today. Each Christmas, every child in the congregation had to take one of their good toys and give it to a poor child. One year, I offered my yo-yo and mother told me that I had to give a better present. At the Christmas service, the minister stood next to the manger, full of donated toys, and said, "It is better to give than to receive." This kind of concrete learning I understood.

The autistic/Asperger's mind tends to dwell in negatives, and this is something parents and professionals should be aware of and find ways to counteract. It is beneficial for a young autistic or Asperger's child to be schooled with positive teachings. One way to do this is through religious training. Helping a child understand what to do, in concrete ways, demonstrating to him or her actions that are giving and positive and helpful to others, can counterbalance this tendency toward negative thinking. If a child asks about something negative, for instance, like stoning as it's mentioned in the Bible, I would recommend parents telling the child that in modern times, people no longer do that. Keep it concrete and simple.

A nice, positive approach for a Christian upbringing would be to give a child one of the WWJD—"What Would Jesus Do?" necklaces or key chains. Then teach the child concrete examples of what Jesus did, or would do, in various situations. For instance, Jesus would not cheat in games. He would not lie, or steal another child's toys. When I was little, I stole a toy fire engine from another child and Mother made me give it back. Moral upbringing must be concrete. A good person is considerate of others. One example I remember from my childhood was being told, by a very sleepy mother, that asking her to open a stuck glue bottle while she was sleeping was not being considerate. Fair play and good sportsmanship are important to teach. Jesus would play fairly and would not be a poor loser. He would not scream and rant if he lost a game. It is unfortunate that in our society today, so many sports heroes behave badly on television and there are no consequences for their actions. It teaches a wrong moral lesson for a child with autism or Asperger's (or any child) to see a famous basketball player not being punished for kicking a TV camera man. If a child views things like this, it is important that a parent tell the child that Jesus would never do that.

Teach your child love and kindness in a concrete manner, with very specific examples. For instance, an example of kindness would be bringing flowers to an elderly lady in a nursing home. There are hundreds of ways parents can share the real essence of their faith with their child with autism or Asperger's, through daily demonstrations of the goodness that is at the foundation of their religion. This is more important, and will help the child in the future more than will learning to recite passages of text, or trying to teach them higher level concepts that they will have difficulty understanding.

Social
Functioning

Chapter

6

Insights into Autistic Social Problems

Learning Social Rules

Emotional Differences Among Individuals with Autism or Asperger's

Healthy Self-Esteem

Four Cornerstones of Social Awareness

✳

The way I see it, a huge mistake
many teachers and parents make is
to try to make people with autism
or Asperger's into something
they are not—turn the geeky nerd
into an ungeek, for instance.

✮

THERE ARE HUNDREDS OF PAPERS IN THE SCIENTIFIC LITERATURE about problems people on the autism spectrum have with social thinking and Theory of Mind (ToM). Theory of Mind is the ability to know what other people may be thinking. In its most elementary form, it's the ability to understand that different people have different thoughts. Involved within ToM is pespective taking, being able to think about and understand an event or a situation "through the eyes of another." These are all social thinking skills that develop without formal instruction in neurotypical individuals, starting at a very early age. These are also skills that most people, including educators, assume exist in all people, to a greater or lesser degree of development. This is not the case within the autism population.

Without a fully functioning social thinking system, individuals with higher functioning autism or Asperger's Syndrome (HFA/AS) stumble along through academic and social situations, missing valuable bits of verbal nuance or nonverbal body messages that are woven into typical conversation. The impairment can be pervasive, even among those with higher intelligence. For instance, a middle school child who can wax eloquent about the anatomical differences among different varieties of alligators may not understand the simple social convention of turning his body towards his conversational partner to indicate interest in what he has to say. In the world of higher functioning autism, neither verbal ability nor IQ are an indication of equal social aptitude and social thinking/reasoning skills. The most basic of social skills may be missing.

Individuals on the more severe end of the spectrum have difficulty with the elementary levels of ToM and perspective taking. I have always been able to pass a simple Theory of Mind test. An example of such a test would go like this. I am in a room with Jim and Bob. Bob puts a candy bar in a box and Jim leaves the room. While Jim is out of the room, Bob moves the candy bar from the box to a desk drawer. When Jim returns, I know that he thinks the candy bar is still in the box. If I had impaired Theory of Mind, I would think that Jim also knows the candy bar was moved to the desk drawer, because I saw him move the candy bar, and if I know it, so does everyone else.

I process this test purely with my photo-realistic visual thinking. I picture Jim outside with the door closed; he could not possibly see the candy bar being moved. When I was given a more complex Theory of Mind test, I did poorly because it required remembering a sequence of several events involving children and an ice cream truck. Plus, the test was presented verbally, which made remembering it even more difficult for my visual thinking mind. My ability to remember spoken word sequence is absolutely terrible. When I ask for directions, I have to write them down to remember the sequence. With the second ToM test, my problem was not in understanding another person's viewpoint, it was with my sequencing skills. Written instructions are best for me, as they are for a majority of children and adults with ASD.

Visual Theory of Mind

My mother taught me starting at a very young age—again, by using visual examples—the importance of understanding how another person feels. When I was about eight, I ate with my mouth open and mother kept telling me to keep it closed when I was chewing my food. She kept telling me to close my mouth, but I still chewed with it open because it made no sense to me why it was important. Then one day I came home from school and I told mother that watching Billy eat with his mouth open made me gag, that it looked like the inside of a garbage truck. Mother quietly replied, "*Your* mouth looks like the inside of a garbage truck when it is open and it makes *me* want to gag." Now I understood that mother was experiencing the same response that I had experienced when I saw Billy chew with his mouth open. To understand how another person felt in the situation, I had to experience myself what the other child was experiencing. For children who are less visual learners and respond well to verbal language, telling them that eating with their mouth closed is a rule may sometimes work.

Avoid Being Abstract

Conversely, it is also difficult for people who think abstractly to understand situations where nonabstract thinking is necessary. This can present career opportunities for people with ASD. In my job designing livestock facilities, nothing is abstract. Abstract thinking is not required to design and build things. This is why I like my career so much. I get a great sense of accomplishment improving the conditions for animals, and now half the cattle in the U.S. and Canada are handled in equipment I have designed. I can see tangible results of my work; it is not abstract. I also get great satisfaction when I can help a parent or teacher solve a problem with a child. When parents tell me that one of my books helped them understand their child and enabled them to work with him more effectively, it makes me really happy.

To be an effective teacher with a child with HFA/AS, explain the rules of living in a nonabstract manner. Do not say to a child, "Well, you have to be good because it is the right thing to do." The words "good" and "right" are much too abstract for the concrete thinking mind of the spectrum child. Instead be specific and say, "You should take turns playing the game because if another child was playing, you would want him to give you a turn to play." Another concrete example would be something like, "Do not steal the other child's toys because you would not like it if he took your things." Teach the Golden Rule, one specific example at a time.

I Am What I Do

Another reason having a good career is so important to me is that I am what I do instead of what I feel. For me, emotional complexity is replaced with intellectual complexity. My greatest satisfaction in life comes from doing things. My best social interactions always involved activities with others with whom I shared a common interest, such as building things or animal behavior. Many of my friends are either in animal behavior, involved with building projects, or work on the animal welfare issue. I also have lots of good friends in the autism community. My career gives my life meaning. This is the way many "techies" feel. To me, intellectual reason and knowledge are extremely valuable. This is why I was so upset ten years ago when the library at our university was flooded. I was upset about books and knowledge being destroyed.

Over the twenty years I have been involved with the autism/Asperger's community, I have learned that some individuals on the spectrum share my way of relating to life and the world, and others do not. There are individuals with HFA/AS who have a few more social emotional circuits connected in their brain, and for them, feelings and emotional connection with others is a bigger part of their functioning. This also, however, produces a greater level of frustration in many parts of their lives, such as friendships and dating. The life of celibacy that I lead would not be right for them. This spectrum of emotional differences in individuals with HFA/AS became even more illuminated for me while working with Sean Barron on our 2005 book, *The Unwritten Rules of Social Relationships*. It was a real eye opener for me to learn that two successful adults with AS can relate to the world so differently, and see where we were almost the same in many ways, and where we were so different. While I am really happy Sean has a girlfriend and a good romantic relationship in his life, that is not a choice that would work for me. Romantic relationships are too abstract for my way of thinking. An article about our differences is included in this chapter.

Sensory-Based Empathy

I can empathize through my senses rather than in a more emotional abstract manner. When I see cattle in the mud, I can empathize with how cold and nasty they feel. One of the things I can really empathize with is physical hardship. When the home mortgage mess in 2007 caused many people to lose their homes, it made me angry. The shoeshine lady at the Denver airport lost her house after she took out an adjustable rate mortgage that she did not understand, and then couldn't meet the escalated payments. When business takes advantage of the poor and less educated of our society, it really makes me mad.

People on the spectrum often have a strong sense of social justice. This sense is probably on a separate brain current from the circuits that are responsible for emotional relatedness between people. This sense of social justice is within me, too. Every time I read another article in the newspaper about people losing their homes due to unethical business practices, it made me furious.

When I took psychology classes in college, I studied Maslow's Pyramid of Needs. At the bottom are food, shelter, and safety and at the top are the abstract ideals of self-actualization, a concept that remains nebulous to me. I am much more concerned about the bottom of the pyramid, those things that affect people's lives on a concrete level, than I am interested in ideology. I understand concrete results. The only ideology that interests me is that which results in real, tangible improvements happening on the ground level. In the autism/Asperger's world, that would be an ideology that produces a good outcome for a child. A nonverbal child should have the opportunities to grow up and have a meaningful life in a group home and possibly hold a job, depending on their level of functioning. People on the higher end of the spectrum should be able to live independently, work, and contribute to society as their own interests and viewpoints dictate. For the really smart Asperger's individuals, a college education and a career is a reasonable goal.

Some of the HFA/AS individuals who feel emotional connectedness, who pursue not just social but romantic relationships, may find success in dating or marrying another person who shares their traits. Socialization through a shared interest, such as a science fiction or history club, are often where the first dates occur. I have talked to many neurotypical spouses who do not understand a husband who is Asperger's. They are concerned about his lack of social emotional relatedness. I explain to them that social skills can be learned like acting in a play. The brain circuits may not be hooked up for emotional relatedness, but he can be a good provider, a good parent, and very loyal. These individuals often possess many good traits, such as honesty, dedication, steadfastness, and a sense of social justice, that can be good in a marriage.

I am a Nerd

The way I see it, a huge mistake many teachers and parents make is to try to make people with autism or Asperger's into something they are not—turn the geeky nerd into an ungeek, for instance. That just won't work. Teaching them to be socially functional is a worthy goal and one not to be overlooked. However, it would be in everybody's best interest to remember that the world is made up of all sorts of individuals, and that geeks, nerds, and people with mild Asperger's are often one and the *same* thing. I can learn social rules, but I will never have the undercurrent of social emotional relatedness that exists in some people. The neural circuits that connect those parts of the brain just aren't hard-wired in me.

I have heard sad stories where a mother took her teenager out of computer classes that he truly enjoyed to place him in situations to make him more social. That was a totally wrong thing to do for two reasons. First, it robs him of the opportunity to develop a talent and interest that can lead to future employment. Second, the teen's social experiences are going to more naturally unfold and progress with the other computer students—those with whom he has shared interests. The happy geeks excel at their jobs and get to work in Silicon Valley where they are appreciated for their brains. The unhappy geeks end up without activities to keep them intellectually stimulated, and instead, are forced into uncomfortable social situations that, more often than not, fail to achieve the goal of making them more social. The people in the world who think that social connectedness is the ultimate goal of life forget that telephones, social networking websites, text messaging, and all the other electronic vehicles that fuel their passion to socialize are made by people with some degree of autism. Geeks swoon over the new technology they create; social addicts swoon by communicating with the technology and showing it off as a status symbol. Is one "better" than the other? I think not.

Dr. Nancy Minshew did a functional MRI brain scan on me that indicated that I was innately more interested in looking at videos of things than videos of people. When I did the scan, I had no idea of its purpose. A series of short video clips of people and things such as bridges, buildings, and fruit were shown. I immediately noticed that the videos were old and scratchy and looked like they came from the 1970s. This triggered my mind into problem-solving mode to figure out where the researchers had gotten these old tapes. The pictures of things provided more clues to the origin of the videos than the pictures of people. When the things flashed on the screen, I looked for cars because I wanted to know how old the videos were. My brain reacted by giving more neural activity to pictures of things than people.

There is no right or wrong in the interests and ways of being among individuals with HFA/AS—provided they can function reasonably well within society. If they cannot, further social learning is clearly needed. However, when all else is relatively equal, the way I see it, parents and educators should respect the innate interests of the child and nurture their expression. Not everyone in the world is highly social, and that's a good thing. It's the same within the autism spectrum. In another case I learned about, a boy with more severe autism was a great artist. His mother was so upset that he would never marry (her dream for her son), she was hesitant to help him develop his artistic ability. For this kid, art was his life. Fortunately, she was persuaded to start a business selling her son's art. He is content to draw all day, and this gives his life meaning.

The autism/Asperger's spectrum is broad. Many individuals are blessed with a unique ability while others do not have any special skills. But each individual, no matter what level of skills or IQ or social abilities, can become a contributing member of the community. This is what will give meaning to their lives. Our goal, therefore, is not to make these individuals find meaning in *our* lives, but for us to help individuals with autism/Asperger's find meaning in their own.

Insights into Autistic Social Problems

A N INTERESTING STUDY BY DR. AMI KLIN AND ASSOCIATES AT THE Yale Child Study Center is helping to explain some of the social problems in people with autism. Both normal and autistic adults were fitted with a device that tracked their eye movements, allowing the researchers to determine what the person was looking at. Subjects wearing the eye tracking device were shown digitized clips of *Who's Afraid of Virginia Wolf,* a movie that contains a high number of instances of social interaction between people in a living room setting. (It is the kind of movie I find boring, because of its social nature.)

The first finding was that autistic subjects fixate on the mouths of people instead of on their eyes. I think one of the reasons they do this is because of their problems hearing auditory detail. I have problems hearing hard consonant sounds. If somebody says "brook" I know the word is not "crook" if it is spoken in the context of a picnic. Looking at the mouth of the person talking makes hearing the correct word easier. I find that when I am in a noisy room, hearing is more difficult if I look at a person's eyes. I tend to point my good ear towards the person, in order to hear better.

Amy Klin's study also showed that a normal person's gaze rapidly switched back and forth between the eyes of the two people conversing in the movie. This happened with less frequency in a person with autism. In one particular test, the subjects viewed three people conversing. The autistic person's gaze switched only once while the normal sub-ject's gaze moved at least six times among the three people on the screen.

This can be explained by attention-shifting delays that are often pres-ent in autism. Research conducted by Eric Courchesne, in San Diego, has shown that autistics take much longer to shift attention between two different stimuli than do their normal counterparts. The inability to shift attention quickly may explain some of the social deficits that develop within this population. Even if a person with autism was more aware of social cues that go on between people, their inability to quickly shift focus would prevent them from catching these short, silent mes-sages that people frequently use to communicate nonverbally.

Processing the meaning of eye movements requires many rapid attention shifts. This may partially explain why people with autism may not even be aware of subtle eye movements that often occur dur-ing conversations. I did not know that people communicated with their eye movements until I read it in a book, in my early fifties. All my life I existed unaware of this part of communication. As a child, I understood that if a person's head was pointed towards me, they could see me. But I did not notice smaller eye movements. Many adults with autism have commented that they finally discovered, at a later age, that normal people have a language of their eyes; however, they could never understand it. Not being able to rapidly shift attention may be the rea-son why.

To help people with autism better participate in conversation, peo-ple can slow down their speech, talk their thoughts out loud in more detail, instead of using nonverbal eye and body language, and check for comprehension by the person with autism, repeating things if needed.

Learning
Social Rules

CHILDREN AND ADULTS ON THE AUTISM SPECTRUM ARE CONCRETE, literal thinkers. Ideas that can't be understood through logic or that involve emotions and social relationships are difficult for us to grasp, and even more difficult to incorporate into our daily lives. When I was in high school, figuring out the social rules was a major challenge. It was not easy to notice similarities in people's social actions and responses because they were often inconsistent from person to person and situation to situation. Over time, I observed that some rules could be broken with minor consequences and other rules, when broken, had serious consequences. It perplexed me that other kids seemed to know which rules they could bend and break and which rules must never be broken. They had a flexibility of thinking that I did not have.

I knew I had to learn these rules if I wanted to function in social situations. If I had to learn them, they somehow had to be meaningful to me, to make sense to me within my own way of thinking and viewing the world. I started observing others as would a scientist and discovered I could group the rules into an organizational format to which I could relate: into major and minor categories. By the time I was a senior in high school, I had a system for categorizing some of the social rules of life. I still use the same system today.

I developed four rule categories: 1) Really Bad Things; 2) Courtesy Rules; 3) Illegal But Not Bad; and 4) Sins of the System.

Really Bad Things

I reasoned that in order to maintain a civilized society, there must be prohibitions against doing really bad things such as murder, arson, rape, stealing, looting, and injuring other people. If really bad things are not controlled, a civilized society where we have jobs, food in the stores, and electricity cannot exist. The prohibition against really bad things is universal in all civilized societies. Children need to be taught that cheating—in all forms, not just on tests—is bad. Learning to "play fair" will help a child grow into an adult who will not commit really bad things.

Courtesy Rules

All civilized societies have courtesy rules, such as saying "please" and "thank you." These rules are important because they help prevent anger that can escalate into really bad things. Different societies have different courtesy rules, but they all serve the same function. In most countries, some common courtesy rules are: standing and waiting your turn in a line, good table manners, being neat and clean, giving up your seat on a bus to an elderly person, or raising your hand and waiting for the teacher to point to you before speaking in class.

Illegal But Not Bad

These rules can sometimes be broken depending upon the circumstance. Rules in this category vary greatly from one society to another and how an individual views these rules will be influenced by his or her own set of moral and personal beliefs. Be careful though: consequences for breaking some are minor; for others, there may be a fine. Included in this category is slight speeding in cars. One rule I often recommend breaking is the age requirement for attending a community college. I tell parents to sign up the child so he can escape being teased in high school. However, the parent must impress upon the child that this is a grown-up privilege and he must obey all the courtesy rules. An example of a rule that would not fall in this category would be running a red light. Doing this carries the possibility of injuring or killing someone, which is a Really Bad Thing.

Sins of the System

These are rules that must never be broken, although they may seem to have little or no basis in logic. They must simply be accepted within our country and our culture. For instance, a small sexual transgression that would result in your name being added to a sex-offender list in the U.S. may have little or no consequence in another country. In the U.S. the two major sins of the system are sexual transgressions and drug offenses. Never commit a "sin of the system" because the penalties are usually very severe.

This method of categorizing social rules has worked well for me. However, each person with autism may need different rule categories that make sense for him or her.

My emotions are all in the present.
I can be angry but I get over it quickly.

✫

Emotional Differences Among Individuals with Autism or Asperger's

I GAINED SOME VALUABLE INSIGHT INTO BOTH MYSELF AND OTHERS ON the autism spectrum when I worked with Sean Barron on our book, *Unwritten Rules of Social Relationships: Decoding Social Mysteries Through the Unique Perspectives of Autism.* There were areas where Sean and I shared similar emotions and other areas where emotional relatedness was experienced almost opposite one another. We both are independent, well-functioning adults, with varied interests and social relationships, yet our social-emotional development took very different paths.

We were similar in two main areas: rigid, black-and-white thinking and singular obsessions. In elementary school, Sean obsessed over the exact angle of parked school busses. My obsession was collecting election and wrestling posters. Both of us bored other people silly talking about our favorite things.

We also shared a rigid thinking style. Sean describes how he built an airplane from Tinker Toys and became enraged when one small, inconsequential part had been left out. Instead of taking pride in his accomplishment and realizing how minor the little part was, he smashed the airplane to pieces. In his mind, you either built the model correctly, or you failed. I had a similar experience when I started

147

designing cattle corrals. One of my early clients was not completely satisfied with my work. I did not realize it is impossible to please everybody. In my mind, his dissatisfaction meant I might have to give up cattle corral design forever. Fortunately, my good friend Jim Uhl, the contractor who built the corrals, talked me into continuing my design work.

Emotionally, Sean and I are very different. I solve social problems with logic and "instant replays" of the mistakes I made, using my strongly visual imagination. I analyze these photo-realistic replays of social missteps as a football coach would analyze his team's maneuvers. My satisfaction in life comes through interests I can share with other people and a challenging career. Sean is a word thinker; he has to figure things out in words and emotions. He feels connected to people via his emotions. Where I replaced emotional complexity with intellectual complexity, Sean strove to gain social-emotional relatedness.

My emotions are all in the present. I can be angry but I get over it quickly. When I replay scenes, the emotions are no longer attached to them. Sean had a lingering, seething anger I do not have. More like so-called "normal" people, he can get angry and it can simmer like a pot on a stove. In our book, Sean describes becoming jealous of his dog's social skills. It made him jealous that his parents and sister responded more positively to the dog than to him. It would have never crossed my mind to be jealous of a dog's social skills.

However, Sean picked up more social cues than I did. If people tolerated me and did not tease or yell, I was satisfied. When I first started visiting feedlots, the cowboys thought I was totally weird. As long as they allowed me to help work cattle, I was happy. Their impressions of me didn't cause me hardship or sad feelings. To fit in within my work environment, I had to prove my worth by being really good at what I did. I sold my skills and work, not my personality. With Sean, the feeling of "being connected" was more important.

Unwritten Rules contains many examples of the social-emotional similarities and differences between Sean and me. However, the basic difference in how Sean and I perceive the world is this: I am what I do and Sean's sense of being is what he feels. In the future, brain scans will be able to identify the differences between individuals' social-emotional functioning. I speculate that Sean, and individuals on the spectrum like him, have a few more social-emotional neural connections in their brain than do I, or individuals like me, with stronger visual, logical processing styles.

✵

(Unwritten Rules of Social Relationships: Decoding Social Mysteries Through the Unique Perspectives of Autism by Temple Grandin, Sean Barron and Veronica Zysk won a prestigious Silver Award in ForeWord Magazine's 2005 Book of the Year competition.)

In the old days, the diagnosis
was gifted, not disabled.
Attitudes strongly influence
how we perceive spectrum kids today.

Healthy
Self-Esteem

ONE OF THE MOST PIVOTAL REASONS I THINK I WAS ABLE TO SUC-
ceed in the neurotypical world as an adult was because Mother
fostered a strong, healthy sense of self-worth in me as a young child. It
wasn't one particular thing she did that other parents didn't do.
Actually, in the '50s and '60s, consciously building your child's self-
esteem wasn't part of the psychology of parenting. Back then kids just
naturally did more things together, especially outdoor activities,
because there weren't video games, DVDs, and computers to capture
solitary attention indoors as there is today.

Even so, I think Mother unconsciously realized two important
things about self-esteem:

- Self-esteem is built little by little through real achievements.
  For instance, when I created beautiful embroidery, that project
  took time, effort, and patience to complete and made me feel
  good about myself.

- The literal, concrete mind of the autistic child requires that self-
  esteem be built through tangible accomplishments, coupled with
  verbal praise.

The "fix it" mentality that seems more prevalent today wasn't part
of my younger years, either. While I did have speech therapy in elementary school, and would visit a psychiatrist once a month, both of

these activities were conducted in a manner that to me didn't feel like something was wrong with me that needed "fixing." Nowadays, kids are being whisked off to one evaluation after another and go from therapy program to therapy program, some five or more days a week. What message is that sending the child other than that parts of him are somehow unacceptable, or that his autism is bad? I think the intellectually gifted child suffers the most. Asperger children with IQs of 140+ are being held back by too much "handicapped" psychology. I have told several parents of brilliant AS children that in the old days, the diagnosis was **gifted**, not disabled. Attitudes strongly influence how we perceive spectrum kids today.

Throughout elementary school, I felt pretty good about myself. I flourished with the many projects I created, the praise they received from family and teachers, the friendships I shared, and the new experiences I mastered. When I won a trophy at winter carnival, that made me happy. When Mother had me sing at an adult concert when I was in sixth grade, I felt good about that. Even during the difficult high school years, my special interests kept me moving forward. I could revert to my hobbies when things got tough socially. It helped me get through those years.

Today, kids are being reinforced for the littlest things. It's setting up a cycle of needing approval for every little thing they do. The *Wall Street Journal* has run many articles lately about young kids entering the workforce who need constant praise from their manager or they can't get their job done. Parents and teachers need to take a look at how they're reinforcing children. As a child ages, the amount of praise he or she receives from others falls off dramatically. A child who constantly receives praise for making efforts into the social arena is going to face a rude awakening later in life, which can negatively affect his motivation to stay socially involved. It's a Catch-22, and one that needs more attention than it's currently being given.

I wasn't praised all the time by Mother or my teachers; far from it. Neither were other kids. We were praised when we did something significant, so the praise was really meaningful and was a strong motivator. The everyday things, such as behaving at dinner, in church, or when we visited Aunt Bella, were not praised. It was just expected that I would behave. But when I made a beautiful clay horse in third grade, Mother really praised that.

Parents can start kids on the road to healthy self-esteem by offering praise associated with something concrete they can see or touch or smell. This has real meaning to the literal, concrete thinking mind of the ASD child. Especially when kids are young, encouraging them to engage in activities with visible, tangible outcomes helps them learn the direct connection between their actions and their abilities, their sense of mastery and control over their world. You can't build things or paint pictures or create anything concrete without making choices, learning sequencing skills, seeing how parts relate to a whole, learning concepts and categories. This, in turn, lays the groundwork for more advanced skills to form, skills indigenous to the less-concrete world of social interactions.

Try building self-esteem in your child from the outside in, starting with tangible projects, and your child will find his own self-esteem blossoming from the inside out.

For me, social thinking skills
largely developed over time
and through repeated experiences.

Four Cornerstones
of Social Awareness

A CHIEVING SOCIAL SUCCESS IS DEPENDENT UPON CERTAIN CORE attributes of the person with ASD. In our book, *Unwritten Rules of Social Relationships*, my co-author Sean Barron and I introduce four aspects of thinking and functioning we think contribute the most to successful social awareness and social interactions. These Four Cornerstones of Social Awareness are:

- **Perspective-taking**: the ability to put ourselves in another person's shoes—to understand that people can have similar or different viewpoints, emotions, and responses from our own. At an even more basic level is acknowledging that people exist and that they are sources of information to help us make sense of the world.

- **Flexible thinking**: the ability to accept change and be responsive to changing conditions and the environment; the mental ability to notice and process alternatives in both thought and actions; the ability to compare, contrast, evaluate.

- **Positive self-esteem**: a "can-do" attitude that develops through experiencing prior success and forms the basis for risk-taking in the child or adult. Self-esteem is built upon repeated achievements that start small and are concrete and become less tangible and more complex.

- **Motivation**: a sustained interest in exploring the world and working towards internal and external goals, despite setbacks and delays.

Often, motivation needs to be encouraged in kids with ASD, especially within the social arena. Let the child feel the benefits of motivation first through using the child's favorite topics or special interests, and then slowly broadening out into other activities. If the child loves trains, teach reading, math, and writing with train-centered books, examples, and activities. Play train-themed games to motivate social interaction.

Based on the social understanding Sean and I have achieved in our lives, we emphatically agree that perspective-taking, being able to look beyond oneself and into the mind of another person, is the **single most important aspect of functioning that determines the level of social success** to be achieved by a child or adult with ASD. Through it we learn that what we do affects others—in positive and negative ways. It's the link that allows us to feel connected to others. It gives us the ability to consider our own thoughts in relation to information we process about a social situation, and then develop a response that contributes to, rather than detracts from, the social experience.

In our book, Sean describes how "talk therapy," as he called it, helped him develop better social thinking skills and appreciate the varied perspectives of other people in his life. During his middle and high school years, he and his parents would sit for hours, sometimes until 1:00 or 2:00 a.m., discussing the most basic concepts of how relationships worked. For instance, Sean explains that even in his late teens, he still didn't understand why it wasn't okay to "absorb" people who took a genuine interest in him and showed they cared about him—that is, why it wasn't acceptable to spend all the time he wanted with someone who was much older and had family and other personal obligations. He couldn't understand why they wouldn't make him the centerpiece of their lives, as did his parents.

For me, social thinking skills largely developed over time and through repeated experiences. The more social data I put on my mental hard drive, the better able I was to see the connections between my own thoughts and actions and those of others. For me, these social equations were born from my logical mind: "If I do X, then the majority of people will respond with Y." As I acquired more and more data through direct experience, I formed categories and subcategories and even more refined subcategories in my social thinking. That's why it's so important for parents to engage children in all sorts of different activities and experiences. Without that direct learning—and lots of it—children don't have the information they need to make these social connections in their thinking.

Perspective-taking works hand-in-hand with flexible thinking; it provides opportunities for experiencing success in social interactions, which in turn fosters positive self-esteem. It can also act as a source of internal motivation, especially as children grow into adults and the type and quality of social interaction expands.

Social *thinking* skills must be directly taught to children and adults with ASD. Parents, teachers, and service providers are slowly starting to realize the importance of incorporating such lessons into the child's overall education plan. Doing so opens doors of social understanding in all arenas of life.

Medications and Biomedical Therapy

Chapter

7

Alternative versus Conventional Medicine

Evaluating Treatments

Medication Usage: Risk versus Benefit Decisions

✴

Little research exists on drug use in children. Doctors and parents need to be doubly careful and consider medications only after other behavioral/educational options have failed to alleviate the symptoms.

✦

TEN YEARS AGO THERE WERE LIMITED THERAPIES AVAILABLE FOR individuals with autism spectrum disorders. Today, that picture is very different. Autism has captured attention within mainstream medicine (pharmaceutical companies) and within the realm of complementary and alternative medicine. One might assume this is good news, and to a degree, it is. As we learn more about the spectrum of autism and the individuals within it, valid, effective treatment options have been developed. However, not all companies have the best interests of individuals with ASD and their families at the heart of their business. Profit motives run deep, and snake-oil salesmen never go away. New interventions with slick public relations and marketing campaigns attached to them lure susceptible parents with promises of overnight success and, in some cases, a cure for autism. While some interventions are touted as based on research, closer inspection may reveal that "research" was done on a handful of individuals, sometimes carefully selected so that the intended results are achieved. Not all research is good research. Now more than ever, parents and caregivers need to be educated consumers of autism treatments and carefully evaluate all treatment options, especially those that sound too good to be true.

The three articles in this section will help guide you in making good medication and biomedical decisions. You must think **logically** about the use of both conventional medications and alternative biomedical treatments such as special diets. In 2006, I completely updated the medical section in my popular book, *Thinking in Pictures*. Rather than repeat information here, I'd like to relate some of my personal experiences with medication and biomedical interventions.

I am one of the many people in the autism community who was saved by antidepressant medication. Throughout my twenties, problems with constant anxiety and panic attacks got worse and worse. I would wake up in the middle of the night with my heart pounding. Going to a new place sometimes brought on waves of panic and I would almost choke when eating. If I had not started antidepressant medication in my early thirties, I would have been incapacitated by constant anxiety, and stress-related health problems. My professional life—the part of my world that brings me so much happiness—would have suffered tremendously.

After consultation and discussion about medication options with my doctor, I started taking Tofranil (imipramine) in 1980. Within a week, the anxiety and panic was 90% gone. No drug can provide 100% control of symptoms and I avoided the temptation to take more of the drug every time I had a minor anxiety episode. Three years later, I switched to Norpramin (desipramine) and it has worked consistently well at the same low dose for over 25 years. Today, one of the second-generation SSRI (Selective Serotonin Reuptake Inhibitor) antidepressants such as Prozac (fluoxetine), Zoloft (sertraline), or Lexapro (escitalapram) would be a better choice. (The use of the newer types of antidepressants is discussed in one of the articles in this section.) Since my old drug still works, I am not going to risk switching it.

To keep my medication working, I also turned my attention to supplemental therapies that improve physical functioning. I started incorporating lots of exercise into my daily regime. I do 100 sit-ups every night. Living in Colorado, and traveling as extensively as I do, light therapy during the winter months is also helpful. I purchased a travel-sized full spectrum light from *www.Litebook.com*. It really helps prevent the dark winter "blues." During the months of November, December, January, and February, I get up at 6:00 in the morning, while it's still dark, and use the light therapy for at least thirty minutes. This extends my photoperiod to be more like summer, which in turn has increased my energy during winter. I feel so much better.

Can I ever stop taking my medication? Countless people cause tremendous problems for themselves when they relapse after quitting an effective medication that had controlled their condition. Sometimes a previously effective medication fails to work when it is restarted. The person can end up in a worse position than before the medication was started. At present, there is a lack of research on long-term management of depression, bipolar disorder, and many other conditions. Funding from pharmaceutical companies mainly pays for short-term studies on medication usage. There is no research to tell me if I can safely stop taking Norpramin now that I am sixty. Since my condition is stable, I do not want to take the risk of experimenting when there is no research to guide me. I am on a single drug and it works. I plan to keep taking it.

I want to emphasize that the autism spectrum is very variable. Some people with high-functioning autism and Asperger's never experience severe enough anxiety, panic, or depression to warrant medication. Their physical nature, their body chemistry, is such that they can remain calm and level functioning. There are others who need some medication to get through puberty and then they can stop taking it. People with minor depression can often wean themselves off medication, especially if they are getting counseling or cognitive therapy in tandem with their drug use. But people with severe depression, bipolar disorder, and people like me—whose body chemistry is out of kilter—are likely to experience major setbacks if they suddenly stop taking medication.

Avoid Medication Problems

A frequent mistake often made with medication use is increasing the dose or adding new medications every time the individual has an aggressive or anxious episode. I repeat an earlier bit of advice: the use of medications is serious business and individuals—doctors and patients—should approach this in a logical, methodical manner. If a drug is no longer being effective, upping the dose is not always the answer. Likewise, every new symptom does not warrant a different medication. A person who is on eight different drugs should probably be weaned off many of them. If they have been on the drugs for many years, one drug at a time should be reduced over a period of months.

Compounding the issue further is that many similar drugs are now available. For example, Prozac and Lexapro are both SSRI second-generation antidepressants. There are various separate yet similar medications in this broad class of drugs. The upside to this is if you do not like one drug, others that address the same symptoms are there to try. The biggest mistake doctors make with antidepressants and the atypical drugs such as Risperal (risperideone) or Abilify (aripiprazole) is giving too high a dose. Over fifty parents have told me their child did really well on a small dose of a drug but became agitated and could not sleep on a higher dose. For many people on the autism spectrum, the most effective dose of antidepressants and atypical medications is much **lower** than the recommended dose on the label.

A good doctor is careful in prescribing medications, changing dosage, or adding new medications to the mix. Parents need to be equally educated in understanding possible side effects, changes in behavior that signal problems, proper administration of the drug, etc. This is especially true when medications are being used with children. Most medication trials are done on adults, and while the symptoms in children may mirror those in adults, their body systems are different. Little research exists on drug use in children. Doctors and parents need to be doubly careful and consider medications only after other behavioral/educational options have failed to alleviate the symptoms. When medication is warranted, sometimes an odd combination of drugs works. (Find more information in *Thinking in Pictures*.) A good rule of thumb is that for most individuals, three or fewer drugs will usually work. This applies only to medication used to treat behavioral issues, such as anxiety, depression, or severe panic, and not to medications needed for epilepsy or other physical/biomedical conditions.

Supplement and Drug Interactions

Many parents assume that vitamins, herbs, supplements, and alternative treatments taken orally are safe because they are not "drugs." This is not true, and caution should be used with these formulations as well. Vitamins are either water-soluble or fat-soluble. Water-soluble vitamins are not stored in the body. The body metabolizes what it needs when taken and excretes the rest through the urine. They need to be replenished on a regular basis. Fat-soluble vitamins, on the other hand, are stored in the liver and fatty tissues in the body, and are eliminated much more slowly. Vitamins A, D, E, and K are fat-soluble. Care should be taken in using these, since they can build up in the system and cause toxic reactions. The body systems of individuals with ASD are often wired differently; their immune systems can be impaired. Parents and doctors should not automatically assume that the recommended dosage on the bottle is appropriate. Trained professionals should be consulted when using any supplement with a child or adult with ASD. Herbs deserve the same cautionary measures, too. While they have been used for hundreds of years, little research has been done on different combinations of herbs or different dosages used for individuals in today's society. Especially when other medications are involved.

The more things used with a child—either conventional or alternative or a combination of both—the more likely a bad interaction will occur at one point. This is the primary reason to try only one medication or supplement at a time, so you can observe its effects before you add another. Some interactions are very dangerous; adjusting doses can compensate for others. One drug may block the metabolism of another. When this occurs, it may cause the same effect as a double dose of the drug because the drug is removed more slowly from the body. This can result in different reactions, ranging from sleepiness to agitation, in different individuals. Even typical food products can affect how the body processes medications, vitamins, or supplements.

For instance, grapefruit juice enhances the effects of many drugs in weird ways while orange juice does not. Some supplements act as blood thinners and too high a dose can cause bleeding. St. John's Wort speeds up drug metabolism and it may render vital drugs such as antibiotics ineffective. I took a soy-based gel cap natural calcium supplement that had strange hormonal effects and made my post-menopausal breasts sore. Now I make sure all my calcium supplements have no soy in them.

Conventional medications can also have serious side effects, among them diabetes or skin rashes. The biggest side effect of the atypical class of drugs is weight gain, and sometimes it is significant. Gaining 100 pounds while on a medication is not an acceptable side effect. For some individuals, weight gain can be controlled by either switching to a different drug or cutting back on high glycemic carbs such as sugared drinks, white bread, and potatoes. *Parents* need to carefully monitor side effects and drug interactions. Doctors see patients only sporadically; parents see their kids every day. Tell your doctor **everything** you or your child is taking, or any time you add something new into the mix, no matter how "safe" you deem it to be.

Biomedical Treatments

For young children under age eight, I would recommend trying some of the biomedical treatments first, before using conventional medications. Reports from parents and individuals on the spectrum indicate that the single most important biomedical treatment to try is a special diet. They are often most helpful for children who have the regressive form of autism, where they lose language at 18 to 24 months. The special diets seem to work best if started when the regression occurs. However, these diets can be tried with individuals of all ages, not just children.

Special diets can help some children and adults with ASD and have no effect on others. There are two basic types: the wheat (gluten) and dairy (casein) free diet (GFCF) and the Specific Carbohydrate Diet. A special diet is non-invasive, and for some individuals, can bring about remarkable positive changes. However, special diets require time and attention, and in many cases, need to be implemented religiously in order to truly ascertain whether or not they work for an individual. Usually a trial of 1-3 months is all that's needed to gauge effectiveness. Some parents notice positive changes after only a few short days on the diet. Others find their child's behavior gets worse for a few days before it turns around and improvements begin. Dedication to "doing the diet" faithfully is needed once one begins. Some parents will try "a little of the diet" and find it doesn't work, when if they had done it completely, the result might have been more positive.

Critics of special diets cite the lack of scientific research to support their use with this population. Literally hundreds and hundreds of parents have reported it works, and a double-blind, placebo-controlled scientific study has been completed. It is impossible to overlook this large (and growing!) body of anecdotal support. Other critics cite the cost of special diets, having to purchase special foods that are often expensive and sometimes difficult to find locally. This doesn't have to be the case, given a little ingenuity on the part of the family. A simple, inexpensive dairy-free and wheat-free diet could consist of rice, potatoes, fresh fruit, vegetables, nuts, eggs, beef, chicken, pork, and fish. The amount of sugar in the diet should be monitored and in most cases, reduced. Olive oil can be used instead of casein-containing butter and all soy products must be avoided. In general, these special diets are healthy ways of eating. Families find themselves eating little of the highly processed refined packaged foods on today's market shelves, and incorporating more fresh fruits and vegetables into their diets. If the GFCF diet works, the child must start taking calcium supplements because he is getting no dairy products.

The Specific Carbohydrate (SC) Diet differs in that wheat is avoided but dairy in the form of yogurt and cheese can often be added back into the eating plan. High glycemic index carbs such as potatoes and rice and most refined sugar sweets are omitted. This eating plan is similar to an Atkins Diet.

My Special Diet Experience

Neither the GFCF nor the SC diet had a positive effect on my anxiety problems. For me, only conventional antidepressants stopped the panic attacks. At sixty, my immune function is getting poor and I started getting constant urinary tract infections and yeast infections. Dietary strategies have worked well for me to control these problems. Plain Dannon Yogurt helped me control urinary tract infections and when yeast problems started, I made up my own simple version of the Specific Carbohydrate diet. I greatly restricted bread, potatoes, rice, and pasta. Drinks full of sugar are totally avoided. To keep the glycemic index down I eat animal protein, either eggs, meat or fish, three times a day and use healthy olive oil on my salad. The animal protein is especially important at breakfast. A breakfast full of low-fat carbs made my yeast infections worse and caused me to get either headaches or light headed before lunch. A good meat or egg breakfast with some fat in it makes me feel so much better. I also never put food in a blender. Eating whole fruit is beneficial because digestion is slower, which also reduces the glycemic index. I also eat lots of vegetables, beans, and dairy products of all kinds. Restricting wheat helps but I eat small amounts so I do not get so sensitive to wheat that I would have to worry about trace amounts. I have one word of warning. Taking most of the "big white carbs" out of my diet at times makes my stomach hurt. When this happens, I have a little rice with my meat, fruit, and vegetables. The food in my diet does not have to be organic, and everything I need can be easily purchased at the regular grocery store.

I love sweets and wine. After I got my yeast infection controlled, I found I could have some full fat ice cream, wine, or dark chocolate if I never ate it on an empty stomach. In addition to watching what I eat, I take 500 mg of Vitamin C, a standard multiple vitamin, B complex,

Vitamin E, calcium with Vitamin D, and an occasional Omega-3. I buy all my supplements at the regular drug store with the exception of the B complex, which is Blue Bonnet 100 from Whole Foods. I have to be careful with Omega-3 because it interacts with Norpramin and I get nose bleeds. The Omega-3 supplements have many beneficial effects, now documented by research studies.

Our knowledge of biomedical treatments and their effect on individuals with ASD is growing almost daily. Some biomedical interventions are easy and relatively inexpensive to try. Others are costly and some, like chelation, should be approached with the utmost caution, since improper administration can result in death. The diets and some of the supplements such as DMG (dimethyglycine) are non-invasive and worth trying. There is a need for good research on biomedical treatments. Until that comes about, parents should carefully weigh the pros and cons of any biomedical option, and add in new biomedical interventions one at a time, in order to be able to gauge effectiveness.

The **sensible** use of **both** conventional and alternative biomedical treatment has worked well for me. Each child and family is different, however, and parents should never use biomedical options or conventional medication because "everyone is doing it." I am a really practical person and knew that if I was going to use an alternative method like a special diet, I had to figure out how to do that without it interfering with my work or my extensive travel schedule, and without costing me a fortune. With some research and planning, parents can find ways to test out various options on their child, too.

Tips on Finding Information

It is best to base treatment decisions on well-done scientific studies that have been published in respected, peer-reviewed medical journals. This is what doctors call "evidence-based medicine." Unfortunately, the majority of options available now for treating the challenges associated with autism spectrum disorders have no or limited evidence of this quality to support them. Parents, nonetheless, are trying these options in their search for ways to help their child. When peer-reviewed research has not been done on a particular treatment option, what's a parent to do? Valuable information can be gleaned by talking to parents, teachers, and individuals on the autism spectrum. The tip on eating meat or eggs three times a day came from a friend who had an uncontrollable yeast infection that could not be stopped with conventional medication. I trust information from sources where there is no conflict of interest with somebody trying to sell me something. This principle applies to both conventional and alternative medicine. Because a professional is an M.D. does not eliminate personal bias, nor less-than-ethical behavior. It is common knowledge now that doctors accept all sorts of "incentives"—including monthly bonuses—for prescribing certain drugs over others. Parents **must** become educated consumers and question, investigate, and evaluate any drug or alternative treatment recommended for their child.

Another principle I use in decision making is that the more expensive, invasive, or hazardous a potential treatment is, the more documented proof I need that it is effective. I will try a simple dietary change based on a friend's recommendation, but I am not going to spend thousands of dollars or do something potentially hazardous because a friend said I should try it. Back in 1980 when I started taking Tofranil to control my anxiety, few doctors knew that antidepressants worked for anxiety and panic attacks. I had read about the early research in a popular magazine. My next step was to find scientific journal articles before I asked my doctor to put me on Tofranil. And even then, it was a decision we discussed and both agreed upon.

Today, finding medical information on the internet is easy. Not all of it is reliable. There is lots of rubbish and hucksters selling snake oil mixed in with the really useful information. To avoid this, you can search scientific articles on Pubmed, Google Scholar, or scirus.com. To find these sites, type their names into Google. Pubmed will give you free summaries of journal articles from the National Library of Medicine. Google Scholar searches scientific information and filters out most commercial websites. Scirus.com is another scientific search site similar to Google Scholar. Some of the websites where parents and patients chat can also provide useful tips and information.

When I cannot find scientific journal articles, I have a rule for evaluating some of the more exotic, expensive, or hazardous treatments. It is the three family or three individuals rule. I have to find three families who can convince me the treatment works after thirty minutes of detailed questioning. The first question I ask is, "Did you start another therapy such as a diet or ABA at the same time you started the treatment X?" If they say yes, I have no way of knowing that the therapy in question worked. The next part of my questioning seeks specific descriptions of behavior changes. I will not accept vague "it made him better" answers. I want specifics such as "within two weeks he went from ten words to over seventy-five words" or "tantrums went from five a day to one a week." If the family cannot provide these kinds of answers, then it is likely the beneficial effect of the therapy is wishful thinking or perhaps came about because of the placebo effect (improvement resulting from the increased attention given to the child during the treatment period). In doing this informal research of my own, I have found not just three, but numerous families and individuals who have obtained positive effects from using special diets, Irlen lenses, and some supplements. For some of the more exotic treatments, I have not been able to find three families; all I find are salesmen. It is important to keep an open mind in considering new biomedical options, or in using conventional medications, but in the end, the adage still applies: "Buyer Beware."

ADDITIONAL READING

Ammingen, G.P. et al. 2007. Omega-3 fatty acid supplementation in children with autism: A double-blind randomized, placebo-controlled pilot study. *Biological Psychiatry* 61: 551-553.

Bock, K., and C. Stauth. 2007. *Healing the new childhood epidemics: Autism, AHA, asthma, and allergies.* New York: Ballantine Books.

Doyle, B. 2007. Prescription for success: Considerations in the use of medications to change the behavior of children or adults with ASD. *Autism Asperger's Digest,* July-August 2007: 18-23.

Grandin, T. 2006. *Thinking in pictures* (Expanded Edition). New York: Vintage/Random House.

Knivsberg, A.M., K.L. Reichelt, T. Hoien, and M. Nodland. 2002. A randomized, controlled study of dietary intervention in autistic syndromes. *Nutritional Neuroscience* 5: 251-261.

Lindsay, R., and M.G. Aman. 2003. Pharmacologic therapies and treatment for autism. *Pediatric Annals* 32: 671-676.

Mertz, G., and E. Bazelon. 2007. When less may be more: Searching for the optimal medication dosage. *Autism Asperger's Digest,* November-December 2007: 52-55.

Alternative versus Conventional Medicine

Many People Make the Mistake of Taking Sides in the Debate about conventional medications versus alternative treatments, such as special diets or vitamin supplements. Being a practical person, I think the best approach is to pick the item(s) from both that work best for you or your child. One of the biggest problems in the autism field is that some specialists become too wedded to their favorite theory. The debate over the benefits of conventional medication versus so-called "natural" or "biomedical" treatments has turned into a hotly contested issue. My advice is to ignore all the rhetoric and logically figure out what works for your child. The way I see it, this is the truly scientific approach to helping your child.

I have observed individuals who responded very well to a combination of conventional medicine and alternative treatments. The most famous case is Donna Williams, an individual with autism who wrote *Nobody Nowhere* and *Somebody Somewhere*. Over the years I have observed Donna at several conferences. During the early years she could not tolerate people clapping, and as soon as her presentation was finished, she would retreat back to her room. Today, she is able to tolerate all the noise and commotion of a big convention center. When I first talked to Donna she told me that Irlen lenses and the gluten and casein free (GFCF) diet had helped to reduce her severe sensory problems. At that time, Donna was an avid believer in the use of alternative methods instead of conventional medications.

At the 2002 world autism conference in Australia, Donna told the audience that she had added a tiny dose, just one-quarter of a milligram, of Risperidal to her daily regime. The combination of a small amount of medicine along with the special diet really brought about additional positive changes for her.

I know another person who was helped greatly by a combination of Irlen lenses, the GFCF diet, and Zoloft. Zoloft was used initially; the lenses were added a year later. The glasses really helped her organize her writing and do better school work. This was not the placebo effect, because initially she thought that colored glasses were "stupid." Today she loves them. About a year after the glasses were introduced, she started the GFCF diet. This resulted in further improvements. Today she still follows a very strict gluten-free diet, but has been able to add dairy products back into her diet. Like Donna, she continues to use conventional medicine, diet, and Irlen lenses.

On the other hand, do not keep adding more and more things into the mix. Taking six different conventional medications is more often harmful than beneficial. Taking every supplement in the health food store is equally foolish. I like the "a la carte" approach. Use a few items from both sectors of medicine that really work for you, discontinue the items that do not. For me, the GFCF diet had no effect on my anxiety, but I prevent a light-headed, dizzy sensation by eating some animal protein, such as beef or eggs, every day. I also take conventional antidepressant medication.

I have found a combination that works well for me. With some experimentation, you can find what works best for you, or your child, too. It's worth the effort.

Evaluating
Treatments

E VERY INDIVIDUAL WITH AUTISM IS DIFFERENT. A MEDICATION OR an educational program that works for one may not work for another. For example, one child may make really good progress on a highly structured, discrete trial educational program. Another child may go into sensory overload in a discrete trial program and make little progress. That child will require a gentler approach.

Most autism specialists agree that many hours of early educational intervention are needed, but they disagree on whether it should be the Lovaas or the Greenspan method. I have observed that the person actually doing the teaching is often a more important part of the equation than is the method. Good teachers tend to do the same thing, regardless of the theoretical basis of the teaching method. They have a natural instinct about what works and doesn't work for a child, and they adapt whatever method they happen to be using accordingly. If you notice that a particular teacher does not get along with your child, or doesn't seem to have that "feel" for working with him or her, then try another teacher.

Change One Thing at a Time

It is impossible to determine if a new diet, medication or educational program is working if several new things are started at the same time. Start one thing at a time. Many parents are afraid to do this because they want to do the best for their child, and fear that "time is running out." In most cases, a short thirty-day trial period is all that is needed between different treatments to observe the effects. Another good evaluation method is a blind evaluation, where the person offering the evaluation does not know a new educational program or a new medication is being tried. For instance, if the teacher at school mentions your child's behavior has greatly improved, that would be a good indication that a new treatment you're trying at home is working (you didn't tell the teacher beforehand about it). With medication, especially, parents must balance risk versus benefit. A good rule of thumb with medication is that there should be a fairly dramatic, obvious improvement to make it worth the risk or the side effects. For example, if a medication reduced rage attacks from ten per week to one per month, that would be a medication that really works. If a medication makes a child slightly less hyper, that may not be enough benefit to make it worth the risk.

Many treatments are now available. Some have been verified by rigorous scientific studies and others have not. Discrete trial educational programs and SSRI antidepressant medications, such as Prozac or Zoloft, are backed by scientific studies. Interventions such as Irlen lenses or special diets have less scientific backing. However, there are some individuals who are helped by these treatments. One of the reasons that some scientific studies have failed to show results may be because only a certain subgroup of people on the autism spectrum will respond to some treatments. Further studies, especially those that will illuminate what interventions are most helpful to different subgroups, are needed.

In conclusion, introduce one new intervention at a time, and keep a diary of its effects. Avoid vague terms such as "my child has really improved." Be specific about the observed changes, either positive or negative, and make entries at least once a day. An example of a well-worded, useful evaluation would be "my child learned ten new words in one week" or "his tantrums went from five a day to one within four days." Good information will help you make good decisions that will help your child in the long run.

Medication Usage: Risk versus Benefit Decisions

T HERE HAS BEEN MUCH PUBLICITY LATELY ABOUT THE HAZARDS associated with certain medications such as antidepressants and pain relieving drugs for arthritis. It has raised concern among parents whose children already use medications and made more ardent skeptics of parents who already are hesitant to use drugs with their child.

All medications have risks. When making decisions about medication usage, the benefits should clearly—not marginally—outweigh the risks. Common sense dictates that drugs with a higher risk of bad side effects should be used more carefully than drugs with a low risk. A reasonable approach for parents to keep in mind is that a drug with a lower risk of side effects should be tried first.

To approach medication decision-making in a logical manner, it is best to follow these four principles. These principles assume that non-drug approaches have been tried *first* and proved unsuccessful in alleviating the challenge.

- Try one medication at a time so you can judge its effect. Do not change educational programs or diet at the same time a new drug is tried. Keeping a journal of the child's behaviors, demeanor and levels of activity can be helpful in spotting side effects and/or assessing the degree of improvement, if any.

- An effective medication should have an **obvious** beneficial effect. Giving a child a powerful drug that renders him only slightly less hyper would probably not be worth the risk. Conversely, a drug that just takes the edge off his hyperactivity, but makes him very lethargic would be equally bad.

- Antidepressants (both SSRIs—serotonin selective reuptake inhibitors—such as Prozac and older tricyclics) and atypical antipsychotic drugs such as Risperdol should be given at lower doses to people on the spectrum than to the general population. Some individuals with ASD need only one-quarter to one-half of the normal starter dose. Many problems with antidepressants are caused by giving too high a dose: insomnia and agitation are two such examples.

- If an individual has been on a medication that is working really well, it is usually not worth the risk to change it for a newer medication. Newer is not always better.

To make good decisions, parents need to know all the risks involved with the major classes of medications. The following examples of risk versus benefit may help.

- Antidepressants—these come with a "black box" label warning of a slightly increased risk of suicidal thinking during the early period of use. This risk usually occurs during the first eight weeks on the drug.

- Atypicals such as Risperdol—the side effects are high weight gain, diabetes, and tardive dyskinesia (Parkinson's Shaker). There is no black box warning on the label, but the risks are actually greater than those associated with antidepressants. Gaining 100 pounds can seriously compromise health, impair mobility, and contribute to social ostracism and low self-esteem. The risks continue and tend to get worse the longer the drug is taken.

In terms of real risk, the antidepressants are safer for long-term health. However, there are some situations where the benefits of Risperdol far outweigh the risk. It is a very effective drug for controlling rage. If it enables a teenager to attend school, live in a group home, or have enough self-control to learn other cognitive forms of behavior management, it could be worth the risk.

Parents must logically assess the risk-benefit ratio when contemplating any form of medication usage with their child. Discuss the medication thoroughly with the child's doctor. Ask the doctor to provide you with a list of possible side effects of the medication. Do some research of your own on the internet to determine how widely and/or effectively the medication has been used with people with ASD. This is especially true when medication is suggested for use with younger children. Physicians sometimes recommend a drug for a child when, actually, the drug has only been proven effective for adults. Ask whether or not research has been done on the effects of the drug with a younger population. That is certainly one of the risks of which you should be aware, but one that is not usually printed on the product literature!

ADDITIONAL READING

Chavez, B., M. Chavez-Brown, M.A. Sopko, and J.A. Rey. 2007 Atypical antipsychotics in children with pervasive developmental disorders. *Pediatric Drugs* 9: 249-266.

McDougle, C.J., K.A. Stigler, C.A. Erickson, and D.J. Posey. 2008. Atypical antipsychotics in children and adolescents with autism and other developmental disorders. *Journal of Clinical Psychiatry* 67, Supplement 4: 15-20.

Parikh, M.S., A. Kolevzon, and E. Hollander. 2008. Psychopharmacology of aggression in children and adults with autism: A critical review of efficacy and tolerability. *Journal of Child and Adolescent Psychopharmacology* 18: 157-178.

Stachnik, J.M. and C. Nunn-Thompson. 2007. Use of atypical antipsychotics in the treatment of autistic disorder. *Annals of Pharmacotherapy* 41: 626-634.

Cognition and
Brain Research

Chapter

8

Lose the Social Skills, Gain Savant Skills?

People on the Spectrum Focus on Details

The Extreme Male Theory of Autism

Detect Babies at Risk for Developing Autism with Head Measurements

Thinking in Details

A Look Inside the Visual-Thinking Brain

Brain Cortex Structure Similar in Brilliant Scientists and Autism

✢

I picture the frontal cortex
as the CEO of a big corporate
office tower. Every office in the
building is connected to him.

✫

COGNITION AND HOW PEOPLE THINK IS ONE OF MY FAVORITE SUB-
jects. Throughout my life I have been fascinated by how my
thought processes are different when compared to other people's. I love
working my mind to figure things out and solve problems because I
am a pure technie nerd. Some people share my fascination, while others are fascinated by the emotional/social part of thinking and
functioning. There are three research centers in the U.S. that have
done some of the most important work on how autistic brains differ
from normal ones. They are Dr. Eric Courchesne's group in San
Diego, Dr. Nancy Minshew and her colleagues at the University of
Pittsburgh, and Dr. Manuel Casanova at the University of Louisville.

There is probably no black-and-white dividing line between a normal brain and the brains of people on the milder end of the autism
spectrum. All brains are comprised of grey matter, analogous to integrated circuits that process information, and white matter that
connects the processor units together. Half the brain by weight is white
matter "computer cables" that connect different regions of the brain
together. In the normal human brain, every region of the brain has
cables that converge on the frontal cortex. This allows seamless merg-
ing of emotions with information stored in different regions. Dr.
Minshew explains that in autism the "cables" that connect feelings to
information may be either absent or underdeveloped.

Visualization of Brain Organization

For me to conceptualize how the brain works, I have to use photo-realistic images. Unless I have a photo-realistic picture, it is impossible for
me to think. After reading copious numbers of brilliant research
papers, I have summarized them by making a pictorial image about
brain functioning. I picture the frontal cortex as the CEO of a big cor-

porate office tower. Every office in the building is connected to him. Brains are highly variable. They can range from one with a highly connected CEO who oversees everything that goes on in the building, to a CEO with weak connections who lets the different departments do what they want. To put it in computer network terms, the brain is a massively interconnected system.

Researchers refer to disorders in the frontal cortex as "executive function" problems, impairing an individual's ability to process and organize information, create plans and sequences and be flexible in their execution, to self-regulate responses, and achieve goals. Two major factors determine how the brain network will function. They are the long distance white matter "computer cables" that interconnect the different brain departments and smaller local cables that interconnect within a department or between nearby departments. Both Nancy Minshew and Eric Courchesne have done numerous brain scan studies that support this model. In autism, there are fewer long distance white matter connections and more local connections. The different brain departments are less interconnected than in a normal brain. As autism gets more severe, the long distance connections between departments located farther away from each other become poorer.

Manuel Casanova's work has shown that the grey matter processor circuits are also affected. The brain's basic processor circuit is called a minicolumn. In people with autism, the minicolumns are smaller. He did some interesting research that showed that the brains of three deceased scientists also had smaller minicolumns, similar to a brain from a person with autism. A brain with small minicolumns has more processors per square inch, and it will be more efficient at processing detailed information.

Cognitive versus Social Brain

Small minicolumns are connected to white matter cables that wire up local "inter-office" communication. Larger minicolumns are connected to big, white matter cables that can connect to far flung offices on different floors of the building. A brain can be wired to either excel at social interactions with high speed connections to the emotion centers, the CEO, and the heads of departments, or it can be wired to favor the techies in the math or graphics department. In the brain favoring local connections, there would be massive cables draped over the tops of a small group of cubicles to wire together computers that are stacked to the ceiling. This would provide the techies with the computers they would need to do really cool graphics or math savant skills.

Thus, one type of brain network is wired to handle high speed social information lacking detail and the other is wired to concentrate on the details. We need detail-oriented people in this world or there would be no electricity, cars, or computers, or beautiful works of music. Detail-oriented engineers make sure the lights stay on and the bridges do not fall down.

People on the spectrum tend to have uneven skills. The local departments in the office building are not wired up evenly because there is a shortage of good computer cables. One department gets wired really well to create ability in art and another department just gets a single phone line. I am a pure techie and having a good career gives my life meaning. I've learned to make the most of the way my brain is hardwired and I don't feel remorse over missing cables into the social parts of my brain. Yet there are other people on the spectrum who have a few more emotional circuits connected than do I, and they get frustrated and depressed over their poor ability to relate at a social level. Everyone in life has a different set of strengths and challenges within a unique personality. Using a popular analogy, some people see the glass half-empty and are pessimists; others see the glass half-full and are optimists. It's no different among people with autism and Asperger's; we still share common personality traits aside from the different ways our brains are wired. Not all the "problems" within autism arise from the autism. Some arise just because of who we are and the personality we each have.

Michelle Dawson, a woman with autism, has teamed up with Laurent Mottron, at the University of Montreal, with research results that clearly show that the intelligence of people with autism has been underestimated. Normal children tested with the Wisc and the Ravens Progressive Matrices will get similar scores on both tests. Autistic children given both tests will get much higher scores on the Ravens, an average of thirty percentile points higher. The Ravens tests the ability to see differences and similarities in a series of abstract patterns.

Nonverbal Autism

Both nonverbal people and fully verbal individuals with very severe sensory perceptual problems report similar experiences. Perception is fragmented or they may see colors with no clear shapes. Sometimes they report that images break up into pieces like a mosaic. In the visual system, there are separate circuits for color, shape, and motion that must work together to form images. It is likely that in very severe autism, even some of the local circuits are not fully connected. Problems in the white matter circuits that interconnect the thinking and movement parts of the brain may explain why some individuals with autism describe themselves as having a thinking self and an acting self that can't always coordinate together.

Nancy Minshew and her colleagues state that in severe autism, there is a huge lack of functional connections between the primary sensory cortex and the association areas. To use my office building analogy, low level employees are able to receive information from outside the building on phones or computers, but they are either not connected or poorly connected to relay that information to many different departments. Teachers and caregivers of individuals with very severe autism often report that the person has some areas of real intelligence even though they are constantly flapping. These brains may be like an entire office building where most of the interdepartmental and outside network connections are not functioning, but off in one corner are a few cubicles of normal employees with one static-filled unreliable mobile phone line to the outside world.

Over the years I have observed that people on the more severe end of the spectrum are often more normal in their emotional/social processing. This can be seen in the writings of Tito Mukhopadhyay (discussed in Chapter 4, Understanding Nonverbal Autism) and others who can type independently and describe their inner world. To use my office building analogy, there are a few employees over in the more emotional and social parts of the office building, in the human service and sales departments, that still have phone lines intact and functioning. However, everything in the techie department is broken.

This idea of interconnectivity problems among the different brain departments explains why the autism spectrum is so variable and no two individuals are the same in their functioning and understanding. It all depends on where the few good computer cables hook up. Courchesne's work shows that there is an early abnormal overgrowth of white matter in autism. As the severity of autism increases, the white matter overgrowth increases. This may leave fewer good computer cables to form long distance connections between departments, and those connections are necessary for the office as a whole to function efficiently and collect information from all sources.

ADDITIONAL READING

Casanova, M.E., A.E. Switala, J. Tripp, and M. Fitzgerald. 2007. *Comparative minicolumnar morphometry of three distinguished scientists.* Autism National Autistic Society, UK (in press).

Casanova, M.E. et al. 2006. Minicolumnar abnormalities in autism. *Acta Neuropathologica* 112: 187-303.

Courchesne, E., and K. Pierce. 2005. Brain overgrowth in autism during a critical time in development: Implications for frontal pyramidal neuron and interneuron development and connectivity. *International Journal of Developmental Neuroscience* 23: 153-170.

Dawson, M., I. Soulieres, M.A. Gernsbacher, and L. Mottron. 2007. The level and nature of autistic intelligences. *Psychological Science* 18: 657-662.

Hughes, J. 2007. Autism: The first firm finding = underconnectivity? *Epilepsy and Behavior* 11(1): 20-24.

Miller, B.L. et al. 1998. Emergence of art talent in frontal temporal dementia. *Neurology* 51: 978-981.

Minshew, N.J. and D.L. Williams. 2007. The new neurology of autism. *Archives of Neurology* 64: 945-950.

Silk, T.J. et al. 2006. Visuospatial processing and the function of prefrontal-parietal networks in autism spectrum disorders: A functional MRI study. *American Journal of Psychiatry* 163: 1440-1443.

Wicker, I. 2005. Autistic brains out of sync. *Science* 308: 1856-1858.

Lose the Social Skills, Gain Savant Skills?

I HAVE ALWAYS THOUGHT THAT GENIUS IS AN ABNORMALITY. IF ALL the genes and other factors that cause autism were eliminated, the world would be populated by very social people who would accomplish very little. The really social people are not going to want to spend the time necessary to create great art, beautiful music, or masterworks of engineering that require a great attention to detail.

Recent studies about the brain are shedding light on how savant skills work. Brain scans done with functional MRI indicate that the visual parts of the brain in people with autism are more heavily used than are other areas during visual tasks.

British researchers Simon Baron-Cohen and colleagues found that people with autism excel at the embedded figures test. In this task, the person must identify a figure such as a triangle that is hidden in a picture. Brain scans of a normal person's brain taken during the time this task is performed show that many different parts of the brain are activated. In the autistic person, only the visual areas are activated.

Savant skills may be explained by the person having direct access to the visual or musical parts of the brain. There is a great similarity between savant skills in art and music and the talents that emerge in older people who suffer from an Alzheimer-like condition called temporal-frontal lobe dementia. This condition is being studied by Bruce Miller at the University of California in San Francisco. Dr. Miller describes cases of people who had no previous interest in art developing art skills. As their language deteriorated, their art became more detailed and photo-realistic. Two paintings published in his journal article looked like museum quality work. Dr. Miller also describes another group of patients who developed musical skills. As the dementia progresses, the patients become more fixated and compulsive about performing their new talent and social skills are lost.

After reading about twenty scientific papers on this subject, I've started developing another theory along these lines about savant abilities. Verbal language skills cover our basic visual, mathematical, and musical abilities. Perhaps the autistic savant creates art, music, or mathematical computation because he has a direct link into the visual or music or math part of the brain. In my own case, I can think in pictures without words. I can access my visual memory directly because it is not masked by verbal words. When I read, I instantly translate what I read into pictures. From my own experience, I can agree with the idea that people with autism directly access primary parts of the brain that are not accessible to verbal thinkers. This idea is supported by Margaret Bauman's research with brain autopsies. It shows that the parts of the brain where procedural memories are stored are intact in people with autism. Procedural memory does not require words. Examples of procedural memory are learning how to do a puzzle or a motor skill like bike riding.

As our understanding grows of how the brain works, one day we may discover that savant skills are resident in every human being, but that the use of language masks our ability to access these parts of the brain. Perhaps then this understanding will promote acceptance of people who, while lacking social skills, can make meaningful contributions to society just the same.

People on the Spectrum Focus on Details

INTERESTING RESEARCH WITH BRAIN SCAN MACHINES IS BEING CONducted by Dr. Nancy Minshew and her colleagues at Carnegie-Mellon University in Pittsburgh. Their research involves looking at thinking patterns of typical people and people with autism or Asperger's and correlating how thinking patterns are reflected in the brain scans. What is most interesting is that the everyday autistic thinking patterns are different in people with autism versus Asperger's.

The parts of the brain that process individual words and the semantics (meaning) of a sentence are different. People with autism tend to focus only on the words in a sentence and when they do, the "word" part of the brain is activated. However, in people with Asperger's, two parts of the brain are activated, the one associated with words, and the second part that processes the meaning of a sentence. Interesting to note is that the brain of a normal person tends to ignore the individual words and focus on the whole meaning of the sentence.

Dr. Minshew theorizes that the ability of people with Asperger's to process both the individual words and the semantics may partially explain their high IQs. It also illuminates why people with autism often have problems with reading comprehension. Because they focus on the individual words, they lose the sequence of the words and therefore their meaning.

Although I may appear very high-functioning, my correct diagnosis is autism, not Asperger's, because I had significantly delayed language development as a child. I too have problems with processing semantics. It is difficult for me to remember sentences that have sequences such as: "Sally went to the store and told Pam to tell Sue to bring the cake over to Ann's house." Even now I would have difficulty answering a question about this sentence. However, my comprehension is excellent for concrete sentences such as "Jim was wearing a red jacket at the ski resort." It is easier for me to comprehend this sentence and remember the meaning because I can form a single picture in my imagination of the sentence. Teachers can help autistic children and adults with reading comprehension by asking concrete questions that do not involve remembering sequences.

To solve problems, I look at lots of details. It is like putting a puzzle together. Imagine you had a 1000-piece jigsaw puzzle in a bag and you had no idea of the final picture. As the puzzle is assembled the picture may become obvious when it is 25% completed. But that happens piece by piece. Without starting with each individual piece and joining it to another piece, then another, we'd never realize what the picture looks like.

Dr. Minshew's research has given me insight into my own thinking. While the typical person tends to think from concept to details, from the whole to the parts, I have to piece together many details to form whole concepts. All my thinking goes from details to concepts. Parents and teachers should keep this style of thinking in mind as they work with children or adults with autism or Asperger's and incorporate this into their teaching patterns.

The Extreme Male
Theory of Autism

Dr. Simon Baron-Cohen, at the University of Cambridge, has discovered that there are significantly more relatives who are engineers in the family histories of people with autism than in typical families. This is true for my family. My grandfather was an MIT (Massachusetts Institute of Technology) trained engineer who invented the automatic pilot for airplanes and my first cousin's son is a successful circuit-board designer.

Baron-Cohen proposes that people with Asperger's (AS) and high-functioning autism (HFA) have extreme male type thinking and social patterns. Normal boys are systemizers and normal girls are empathizers. "Systemizing is our most powerful way of understanding and predicting the law-governed inanimate universe. Empathizing is our most powerful way of understanding and predicting the social world."

Table 1 is a simplified chart of Baron-Cohen's classification of the male and female thinking patterns. Most normal boys and girls will have traits of both types of brains, with a wide variation among people.

By looking at my own experiences, I can relate to this idea that autistic brains accentuate male traits. As a child I hated dolls and loved to build things. As an adult, I work in the construction industry. Many activities that girls normally like, I hated. I also have the male finger pattern: my ring finger is longer than my second finger.

Normal boys value competition and power more than do girls. If an autistic brain is hyper-male, this would explain why teaching turn-taking, sharing, and fair play should be an essential part of an autistic child's education. When I was a child, my nanny played many turn-taking games with me and emphasized the importance of good sportsmanship and fair play.

Many people have wondered why HF autistic and AS girls often make a better social adjustment. One AS woman suggested that to her, she was like a normal male. If Baron-Cohen's theory is correct, an AS girl may be more like a normal male, but an AS boy would be an extreme male mind. This would be an important and highly relevant insight in designing appropriate social skills programs for both boys and girls.

There is one trait where Baron-Cohen's theory does not hold up. Athletics is a male trait yet many AS and high-functioning people are clumsy and poorly coordinated. Perhaps this involves a deficiency in another area of their brains. Or, perhaps while they have the male mind, their body in most cases is not as extremely developed.

Table 1. Brain Types

MALE BRAIN Systemizing	FEMALE BRAIN Empathizing
• Competition	• Sharing; turn-taking
• Poor theory of mind	• Better theory of mind
• Values power	• Values relationships
• Active aggression	• Indirect aggression
• Self-centered	• Negotiation
• Poorer reading facial expressions	• Better reading faces
• Good visual spatial skills	• Poor visual spatial skills
• Construction toy play	• Interpersonal play
• Mechanical ability	• Ability to empathize
• Discusses objects and activity	• Discusses feelings
• Categorizes things with rules	• More generalization skills

Detect Babies at Risk
for Developing Autism
with Head Measurements

RECENT RESEARCH* INDICATES THAT THERE IS EARLY ABNORMAL overgrowth of the brain in very young children with autism. Eric Courchesne and his colleagues at the School of Medicine, University of California, report that it may be possible to identify babies at risk for developing autism by measuring the size of their heads.

According to Dr. Courchesne, the brain overgrowth occurs before the onset of obviously abnormal behaviors. Autistic babies have a burst of abnormal brain overgrowth prior to twelve months and then there is an abnormal slowing of brain growth.

Measurements show the circumference of the head was abnormally enlarged in infants at twelve months of age. In two and three-year-old children with autism there was still as much as a 20% enlargement. In teenagers and adults, however, it is more difficult to detect differences in head or brain size, as the differences *decrease with age.*

This research is exciting because a simple tape measure could be used as a screening tool for autism in twelve-month-old infants. The head measurements could then be compared to standard charts for normal head size. This early detection, even if viewed only as a warning indicator, would make it possible to start educational and treatment interventions early, when the chance for making positive gains in a child is high. Autistic children need to be kept engaged and this early detection would provide the opportunity for these children to be given extra attention in their interactions with adults. Simple games like Peek-a-Boo and talking to the baby, activities that foster social interaction, may be helpful, as might gentle sensory stimulation, like rocking or holding the baby. While not drastic, this extra attention may help cement foundation learning skills in the very young child that will positively affect his/her ability to continue to learn from other interventions, should the more typical characteristics of autism become noticeable.

Dr. Courchesne has also done computerized brain scans that measure the amount of grey matter and white matter overgrowth in the brain. He found that the back of the brain, where vision is processed, was normal. However, the frontal cortex had the most abnormal overgrowth. This was another very interesting finding, explained Dr. Courchesne, in that the parts of the brain that are most abnormal in individuals with autism are the same parts of the brain that differentiate people from chimpanzees. I find this interesting in that it suggests that something has gone wrong in the mechanisms that control the patterns of growth in the human brain. Discoveries such as these provide important clues in helping us understand where the cause or causes of autism will eventually be found.

�֍

* Presentation: November 2002 by Dr. Eric Courchesne at the World Autism Conference in Melbourne, Australia.

REFERENCE

Courchesne, E. 2004. Brain development in autism: Early overgrowth followed by premature arrest of growth. *Mental Retardation and Developmental Disabilities* 10: 106-111.

Postscript 2008

Since writing this column, there has arisen another simple test for determining if a baby is at risk of becoming autistic. It is observing whether or not the child exhibits joint attention. Joint attention involves sharing one's experience of observing an object, person, or event with another, by following pointing gestures or eye gaze. This skill typically develops around twelve months of age. Normal babies and young children will orient and look at something a mother or teacher is looking at. Some examples of joint attention are when a baby looks at a toy that mom is looking at. The baby's head will turn towards the toy when the mom looks at it and says, "Look at the pretty birdie!" On many flights, I have observed that one-year-old babies will immediately orient and look at me when I wave and say hi. In children later diagnosed on the autism spectrum, joint attention is often missing from their behavior. Another red flag of possible developmental problems is when babies do not respond to peek-a-boo games. Activities such as these that require social interaction are not possible without good joint attention skills. Joint attention is an important developmental milestone in a child and is critical for further development of social, language, and cognitive skills.

It takes careful observation
and keen detective work sometimes
to figure out the detail that
the child uses as an identifier.

Thinking in
Details

HILDE DE CLEREQ, WITH THE CENTER FOR TRAINING ON AUTISM in Belgium, presented great insights into autistic thinking in her presentation at the 2002 World Autism Conference in Melbourne, Australia. As a mother of an autistic child, she observed that her baby reacted to her differently than did her typical child. Her baby recognized her by the smell of her perfume or the color of her dress. If the dress or the perfume were missing, her baby did not recognize her. Autistic babies and children tend to focus on details that may not be relevant or easily discernable to parents or educators.

In my own case, I was able to figure out relevant visual or auditory details, which made it possible to form concepts—such as *dog* and how that concept was different from *cat*. It is my opinion that most people with autism notice far more details in any given situation than do people without autism. It is how we process our world, how we gather information in order to form conclusions. In forming the concept *dog*, I discovered that all dogs have the same type of nose, and can also be differentiated from cats by the sound of barking, rather than meowing.

In more severe cases of autism, a child or adult may become fixated on a detail that is not relevant. Although this detail may provide information to the child or adult, it does not aid as a clue in differentiation. Dr. de Clereq described a boy who was using the toilet properly at home but would not use it at school. He would only use the toilet if the seat was black, a detail that had meaning to him but did not aid in forming the concept of *toilets*. For him, a toilet with a white seat was not recognized as a toilet. It takes careful observation and keen detective work sometimes to figure out the detail that the child uses as an identifier. After the boy's teachers figured out that the color of the seat was the identifying detail, they easily taught the boy to recognize other toilets by covering the white toilet seat with black tape. Gradually they removed strips of the tape and he was able to use toilets with white seats.

In another case, a child became afraid of all red objects after he cut himself with a knife with a red handle. He had made the wrong association with color instead of with the category of sharp objects.

Normal children tend to over-generalize. A good example is all drinking vessels are called "cups." However, the autistic child has difficulty finding the perceptual links for generalization. Some people with autism also have visual processing problems that further impact how information is processed. For many, it is difficult to see large objects, such as a tree or a house. The image fractures into a mosaic or is seen in fragments, like in a kaleidoscope. For others, curves present problems, or depth perception is missing, with all images seen on one flat plane. Sometimes it is easier for a child to look at smaller objects, such as eating utensils, to teach generalization. It can also help to keep backgrounds simple. For individuals with severe sensory processing problems, it may be easier to teach generalization by the feel or texture of objects. Touch provides more accurate information to their brains than does vision or hearing.

A Look Inside the
Visual-Thinking Brain

I RECENTLY HAD THE OPPORTUNITY TO PARTICIPATE IN A BRAIN SCAN study with Dr. Nancy Minshew's research group at the University of Pittsburgh. The MRI scanner was equipped with the latest technology called Diffusion Tensor Imaging, which made it possible to see large white fiber tracts that connect different brain regions together. Two weeks later when I received a copy of my scan, it was a real mind-blower. Compared to my age and sex-matched control, I have two huge broadband-internet-like connections that start deep within my visual cortex and run the entire length of each hemisphere. The normal control subject had the same circuits, but mine are almost twice as thick. Similar findings were discovered in some other young adults with autism. I thought, "Wow, this explains my thinking in pictures." Dr. Minshew and her colleagues are doing groundbreaking research that will help both parents and professionals better understand how people with autism perceive the world.

In another study, Rajesh Kana and other scientists at the Center for Cognitive Brain Imaging at Carnegie Mellon University conducted a brain imaging study that showed that in people with autism, nonvisual material is processed in the visual parts of the brain. Individuals with autism and control subjects were presented with sentences that had either high or low visual imagery. An example of a high visual imagery sentence is "Animals and minerals are both alive, but plants are not."

An example of a low visual imagery sentence is "Addition, subtraction, and multiplication are all math skills." While in the scanner, the subject's task was to press a button to answer whether the question was true or false.

Both of the sentences triggered vivid images in my mind. The first sentence triggered pictures of dogs, cats, cows, corn fields, trees, and crystals. The nonvisual imagery sentence triggered a picture of my third grade arithmetic class. The study results showed that the autistic group activated their visual areas in both types of sentences and the controls activated the visual areas primarily in response to the high imagery sentences. People on the autism spectrum also use the frontal cortex area of the brain much less compared to normal people when performing a visual rotation task. They rely more on non-frontal cortex areas of the brain.

I did horribly on some test tasks labeled as visual that required use of working memory and quick response time—two of my worst skills. Dr. Minshew tried a test on me called Finger Windows. In this task the subject watches the experimenter point to different pegs on an array of pegs laid out on a grid. The task is to imitate the pattern after the experimenter stops pointing. I failed this test. I could remember only three pegs in the correct location and sequence. This was just like my problems asking for driving directions. If there are more than three steps, I have to write them down; otherwise, I cannot remember the sequence. In a series of cognitive tests, the Finger Windows test was most accurate in separating autistic from normal subjects, as there was no way to use an alternate strategy to perform the task. My performance on the verbal digit span test, however, was good because I kept repeating it back out loud. This strategy compensates for my working memory deficit.

What can parents and teachers learn from this research? First, if a child is a visual thinker you cannot get the pictures out of his head. They are his "native language," rather than words. Second, avoid long strings of verbal sequencing when teaching or working with a child.

Keep instructions short and concrete. If the child can read, write the instructions down instead.

REFERENCES

Kana, R.K. et al. 2006. Sentence comprehension in autism: Thinking in pictures with decreased functional connectivity. *Brain* (in press). Advanced access online preprint.

Koshino, H. et al. 2005. Functional connectivity in an MRI working memory task in high functioning autism. *Neuroimage* 24: 810-821.

Silk, T.J. et al. 2006. Visuospatial processing and the function of prefrontal-parietal networks in autism spectrum disorders: A functional MRI study. *American Journal of Psychiatry* 163: 1440-1443.

Williams, D.L., G. Goldstein, and N.J. Minshew. 2006. The profile of memory function in children with autism. *Neuropsychology* 20: 21-29.

Today's "always connected" society has put more social demands on people, and a lack of social ability may be seen as more of a handicap than in the past.

✪

Brain Cortex Structure Similar in Brilliant Scientists and Autism

U NTIL RECENTLY, RESEARCHERS HAD ASSUMED THAT THE BRAIN'S cortex, where information is processed, was not affected by autism. Research by Dr. Manuel Casanova at the University of Louisville shows that both people with autism and three deceased brilliant neuroscientists have similarities in the structure of the cortex. One of the brains studied came from Norman Geschwind, who was a leader in understanding how the brain functions.

The grey matter of the cortex is filled with thousands and thousands of long, slender circuits called minicolumns. Each minicolumn is a group of neurons that form the brain's basic information processing circuit. Both the scientists and people with autism have a larger number of smaller minicolumns per square inch of cortex compared to normal people. To put it in electronic terms, their brains have a greater number of integrated circuits on the "chip."

The size of the minicolumns gives the brain developmental flexibility to favor either efficient processing of social information or efficient processing of detailed information for complex problem solving. A brain can form either fast, efficient processing of information between different, distant regions or fast, efficient processing of information in a local region. Brains with smaller minicolumns have more pathways that interconnect local circuits.

There is a trade-off between having better processing of detailed information and the brain's ability to handle social functions. Social functions, such as interpreting faces, require long distance connections from the frontal cortex to many other parts of the brain. Brains that have fewer larger minicolumns per square inch have more abundant long-distance connection in the brain's white matter between different brain regions. However, their brains are poorer at processing detailed visual, numerical, or factual information.

There is no black-and-white dividing line between normal and abnormal brain structure, and there would be a wide range of brain wiring that would be considered normal. Only one of the scientists in this study had true Asperger's traits. In more severe autism, it is likely that the minicolumns become so small, numerous, and overcrowded that they start to malfunction. This is likely to be one cause of epilepsy and sensory sensitivity problems.

I have often thought that people on the mild end of the Asperger's spectrum may have fit in better years ago than they do today. An eccentric stone mason who designed a cathedral would be admired for his work. A brilliant scientist who preferred the company of mice to humans might have been considered eccentric, but not necessarily labeled socially dysfunctional. In many ways, today's "always connected" society has put more social demands on people, and a lack of social ability may be seen as more of a handicap than in the past.

REFERENCES

Casanova, M.F., A.E. Switala, J. Trippe, and M. Fitzgerald. 2007. Comparative minicolumnar morphometry of three distinguished scientists. *Autism* 11: 557-569.

Casanova, M.F. et al. 2006. Minicolumnar abnormalities in autism. *Acta Neuropathology* 112: 287-303.

Adult Issues
and Employment

Chapter

9

Employment Advice: Tips on Getting and Holding a Job
Happy People on the Autism Spectrum Have Satisfying Jobs or Hobbies
Inside or Outside? The Autism/Asperger's Culture
Going to College: Tips for People with Autism & Asperger's
Can My Adolescent Drive a Car?
Wall Street Journal Social Stories
Innovative Thinking Paves the Way for AS Career Success
The Link Between Autism Genetics and Genius

Parents hold primary responsibility in making sure their children learn basic skills that will allow them to function within society as adults.

✵

I FIRST STARTED DOING TALKS ON AUTISM IN 1986 AFTER MY FIRST book, *Emergence: Labeled Autistic* was published. Over the last 20+ years, I have observed that services for children and individuals on the more severe end of the spectrum have greatly improved. Unfortunately, some individuals on the mild Asperger's end of the spectrum may be doing worse today as children, and especially as they become teens and adults. Why is this so? One reason is that we tend to give attention to those individuals who are the most needy. Individuals who are higher functioning, with language and often good academic abilities, can be easily overlooked as not as much "in need" of services in the school system. That's a fallacy, of course, but nevertheless, the perception that Asperger's types can "get by" on their own is still prevalent within our educational system. Educators don't seem to understand the pervasive nature of social skills impairments, generally because no one has to teach a neurotypical person the basics of social thinking and perspective taking. It just happens as a natural part of development.

Second, there are no mandated services for people with ASD as they age out of the public school system. Once a student reaches 21, options for further education and training are severely limited. Those who are not transitioning on to college or employment are left with little help in the way of structured programs. Some options do exist through Vocational Rehabilitation agencies for day programs or job training programs, but quality services are few and far between, and often have long waiting lists. Remember: Asperger's is a relatively new disability and as the children of yesterday become the adults of tomorrow, agencies are scrambling to catch up with the need for programs and services to address this growing population.

I also notice another issue that makes the transition to employment and adulthood difficult for people with ASD—one that affects this group as deeply as does the lack of services. The way I see it, many of the challenges within this population arise from the less rigid style of child rearing that is prevalent today. During the 1950s, *all* children were taught manners and social rules and "behaving." Mothers made sure their children learned to say "please" and "thank you," knew how to play with other kids, and understood appropriate and inappropriate behavior. There were hard and fast rules to behavior back then, and consequences to acting out were more strictly enforced. Plus, the majority of mothers didn't work outside the home; they had more hours to spend in raising a child and smoothing out problems. Contrast that with the looser family structures and the watered down emphasis on social niceties that is prevalent in today's society. In many families, both parents work. Proper etiquette is no longer viewed as "essential" education as it once was. Social rules have relaxed and "Miss Manners" has been replaced by a tolerance for individual expression, whether or not that expression is socially appropriate. I don't find many of these changes to be positive, but the scientist within me acknowledges that they are very real forces affecting our population. These shifting, changing social rules (or lack thereof) make it more difficult for most people with ASD to understand the social climate around them and learn to fit in. Many arrive at adulthood without even basic daily living capabilities—even children on the higher functioning end of the spectrum. They can't make a sandwich, write a check, or use public transportation. Functional life skills have been neglected. Why that is, only each individual family can say for sure. But in general, this lack of attention to teaching basic life skills while children are young and growing, is having increasingly negative repercussions on people with ASD. Quirky friends I had in college, who would be diagnosed with Asperger's today, all got and kept decent jobs because they had been taught basic social skills while they were growing up. They might still be quirky, still considered eccentric or odd by some, but they could function within society. One Ph.D. I know is underemployed, but has kept full-time jobs with full health benefits his entire life.

In the meat industry where I work, there are older undiagnosed people with Asperger's who have good jobs, with good pay, working as draftsman, engineers, and mechanics. Their early upbringing gave them a foundation of basic skills, so they knew how to act socially, be part of a group, get along with others, etc. Today I see younger individuals with Asperger's who are just as intellectually bright getting fired for being regularly late to work or telling their bosses they won't do something required of their position. When I was little, I was expected to be on time and be ready for school; and I was. Failure to live up to my parents' expectations resulted in a loss of privileges, and my mother was good at making consequences meaningful enough that it made me behave. As I see it, some of the problems these teenagers and adults exhibit—being constantly defiant and not doing what the boss tells them—goes back to not learning as children that compliance is required in certain situations. They never learned when they were six or eight that sometimes you have to do things that parents want you to do, such as going to church or having good table manners. You may not have liked it, but you still did it.

In light of this shifting sea of social skills and social expectations, how can parents and educators better prepare children to become independent, functioning adults while living in today's society? And what can we do to help the adults with autism or Asperger's who find themselves with adequate technical skills, but are unemployable from a social perspective? We start by recognizing that changes need to be made. We need to be realistic with these individuals and our own roles in shaping their lives. We need to focus on talents, rather than deficiencies. Parents hold primary responsibility in making sure their children learn basic skills that will allow them to function within society as adults. This may sound harsh, but there's just no excuse for children growing into adults who can't do even basic things like set a table, wash their clothes, or handle money. We all make choices in our lives, and choosing to make the time for a child with Asperger's to learn functional skills should be at the top of every parent's priority list.

A child's future is at stake—and this should not be a negotiable item. Yet, for some reason, with a growing number of parents, that choice is not being made.

Our public education system also bears responsibility for preparing children to be independent adults. The needs of students with ASD go beyond merely teaching academics. They need to be taught to be flexible thinkers, to be social thinkers, to understand group dynamics, and be prepared to transition to adult life—whether or not that includes college or technical school—with functional life skills that neurotypicals learn almost by osmosis. Education of people with ASD goes far beyond book learning. They absolutely require "life learning" also.

Develop Abilities into Employable Skills

Parents, educators, and teachers need to work on using an individual's areas of ability and interest and turning them into skills that other people want and appreciate. When I was eighteen, I talked constantly about cattle chutes. Other people did not want to hear me go on and on about the subject, but there was a very real need for people to design those cattle chutes. The adults in my life turned my obsession into the motivation for me to work hard, get my degree and have a career in the cattle industry.

In the Education chapter of this book is an article on the three different kinds of cognition in autism and Asperger's. The *visual thinkers*, like me, who think in photo-realistic pictures, are good at jobs such as industrial design, graphics, photography, art, architecture, auto mechanics, and working with animals. I was terrible in algebra and I am noticing more and more visual-thinking students with similar challenges. Many of these kids fail algebra and yet find higher math easy. They need to skip algebra, and go right to geometry and trigonometry. I was never exposed to geometry because I failed algebra.

The music and math minds are *pattern thinkers* who are often good at music, engineering, computer programming, and statistics. Reading is often their weak area. The *verbal word thinkers* who love history are often good at jobs such as legal researcher, library science, journalism, and any job that requires good record keeping. They tend to be really poor at drawing and visual skills. Most children will usually fit into one of these three categories, but there are a few who may not. Some kids have mixed learning styles, sitting halfway between the categories. One lady I know who falls into the music and math pattern thinking category, understands music from a cognitive standpoint but is too uncoordinated to play an instrument. Many pattern thinkers see visual patterns in the relationship between numbers, but she does it all with sound patterns because she has almost no ability to think in photo-realistic pictures the way I do. She has been employed for years doing computer programming.

I also want to emphasize that if a ninth grader is capable of doing university math, he should be encouraged to do it. A person with this advanced level of academic thinking forced to do the "baby math" of his peer group will quickly get bored and uncooperative. Focus on the areas of strength and develop them to their fullest expression. A child may be able to keep at grade level in one subject but may need special education in another. Autism is nothing if not variable.

Getting in the Back Door

Over the years, I have observed that some of the most successful people on the spectrum—those who found good jobs and kept their jobs—entered through the back door. They had parents or friends who recognized their talents and learning profile and then capitalized on their strengths by teaching them a marketable skill, such as computer programming or auto mechanics. I got in the back door by showing potential clients pictures and drawings of cattle handling facilities I had designed. I went directly to the people who would appreciate my work. Had I started my job search in the traditional way, with the personnel office, I might never have been employed. Back then my workplace social skills were underdeveloped, my personal hygiene was poor and my temper flared regularly. People respect true talent and demonstrated ability. A budding architect who brings in a fantastic building model or has a strong portfolio of projects he has completed will attract attention. Employers will become interested in working with people who have ability, even when they exhibit some social skills that are less than on par with their peers. The more special or specialized the talent, the more willing a potential employer may be to accommodate some differences. However, that is not the case for individuals with only marginal talents. That's why parents and educators need to focus on developing emerging talents to their fullest potential. This provides individuals with the best possible chance of securing a good job in their field, despite their social challenges.

The same principle applies to individuals who are on the lower end of the spectrum. Many successful employment placements are made in local businesses that recognize the benefit of having an individual who will be a dependable, solid employee. People who are nonverbal know the difference between doing useful work that other people really need and appreciate, and stupid "busy work." One therapist could not figure out why her nonverbal client kept having a tantrum when she was teaching him to set the table. He was throwing a fit because he was asked to repeatedly set the table and then unset it, without ever eating. The therapist favored teaching skill acquisition over teaching functionality. A better way to teach table setting is to set the table, eat, and then clean up. All people want to feel their efforts matter, and individuals with ASD are no different. We are learning that a lack of verbal communication does not always equate to impaired mental functioning. Even when it does, individuals can be trained to be contributing members of society. Some of the jobs suited to nonverbal persons are stocking shelves, jobs that involve sorting items, gardening work, landscaping, and some factory assembly jobs.

All individuals on the spectrum, from the brilliant scientist to the person who stocks shelves, find multi-tasking difficult if not impossible. If I had to be a cashier in a busy restaurant, it would have been impossible to make change and talk to customers at the same time. Even today I have difficulty with multi-tasking and need to work through one thing at a time. For instance, I can't make breakfast, talk on the phone and do laundry all at the same time.

Parents and teachers, and persons with ASD themselves, need to constantly look for the back door that will open up broader opportunities and employment options. Sometimes these chances can be right in front of you but you do not see them. My first entrance into a big meat plant came about when I met the wife of the plant's insurance agent. That one meeting became the connection I needed to get my foot in the (back) door.

Community colleges have all kinds of wonderful courses for different careers. Many students have found great teachers who served as mentors, both while they were in public school and afterwards. Some parents of talented artists on the spectrum who cannot live independently took entrepreneurial courses so these parents could run a business selling their child's work. Opportunities are available, with a little creative thought and a willingness to work outside the normal boundaries of education and employment.

✳

ADDITIONAL READING

Grandin, T., and K. Duffy. 2004. *Developing talents.* Shawnee Mission, KS: Autism Asperger Publishing Company.

You simply cannot tell
other people they are stupid,
even if they really are stupid.

✻

Employment Advice:
Tips for Getting
and Holding a Job

Grooming

WHEN YOU FIRST MEET WITH A PROSPECTIVE EMPLOYER, DRESS neatly. Your hair should be combed and your clothes must be clean. When I got my first job at a cattle feedlot construction company, I was a slob. Fortunately, my boss recognized my talents and had his secretaries work with me on grooming. Not everyone will be that fortunate; make sure you have good grooming skills.

Sell Your Work

I got my first job because the technical people at the company were impressed with my ability to design cattle handling equipment. Many people with autism and Asperger's do poorly at a job interview with the personnel department. You need to locate the technical people and show them a portfolio of your work. In the 1970s, when I was just getting started with my cattle equipment design business, I always carried with me a portfolio of pictures and drawings.

People respect talent. You need to be trained in an employable field, such as computer programming, drafting, or accounting. The technical professions offer more opportunities for employment and are

217

overall well suited to the autism/AS style of thinking. Show a prospective employer a portfolio of computer programs, engineering drawings or a sample of complex accounting projects. It will help.

Dependability

You need to be punctual and show up for work on time. That also goes for being on time for scheduled meetings during office hours. Employers value dependable employees.

Visual Difficulties at Work

Some people with autism or Asperger's have difficulty tolerating fluorescent lights. They can see the sixty-cycle flicker of the lights and it makes the office environment flash like a disco. A simple way to prevent this is to bring in a 100-150 watt incandescent lamp for your desk. This will greatly reduce the flicker. The use of a flat panel computer display or a laptop is sometimes easier on the eyes than a TV-type monitor. Some people find reading easier if they print text on tan, gray, light blue, or other pastel paper to reduce contrast.

Sound Sensitivity Problems at Work

The noise and commotion of a factory or office is sometimes a problem for people with sound sensitivity. You may want to ask that your desk be located in a quieter part of the office. Headphones or earplugs can help, but you must not wear them all the time. Earplugs worn all the time may make the ears more sensitive, so they *must* be removed when you get home.

Diplomacy

I learned some hard lessons about being diplomatic when I had my first interactions with people at work. Some senior engineers designed a project that contained some mistakes that were obvious to me. Not knowing any better, I wrote a letter to their boss, citing in great detail the errors in their design, and calling them "stupid." It was not well received. You simply cannot tell other people they are stupid, even if they really are stupid. Just do your job and never criticize your boss or other employees.

Freelance Work

This is often a good way to work because it avoids many of the social problems. When I design equipment, I can go into the plant, get the project done, and then leave before I get involved in complex workplace politics. The internet makes freelancing much easier. If you can find a boss who recognizes both your strengths and social limitations, this will make life on the job much easier.

Being Too Good

Several people with autism or Asperger's have told me that they got into trouble with coworkers at a factory because they were "too good" at assembling "widgets." The problem of employee jealousy is a difficult thing to understand, but it exists in the workplace. The boss likes the hard worker, but the other employees may hate him or her. If coworkers do get jealous of your work, I found that it is helpful to try to find something they have built or done that you can genuinely compliment them on. It helps them feel appreciated and that they, too, have done a good job.

Avoid the Peter Principle

The Peter Principle states that people have a tendency to rise to their level of incompetence. There have been several sad cases where a good draftsman, lab technician, or journalist with autism or AS has been promoted into management, and then fired because the social situations just got too complex. The person with autism or Asperger's is especially vulnerable to being promoted into a job they cannot handle because of the social issues. It may be best to politely tell your boss that you can use your skills best in your present position.

219

Be Nice and Have Good Manners

People who are polite and cheerful will have an easier time getting along at work. Make sure you always say please and thank you. Good table manners are a *must*. Greet your fellow workers at least once each day and actively try to engage in some small talk with the people you work with most closely. While it's not necessary to form friendships with everyone you work with, some social interaction is needed if you are to be viewed as part of the group.

Workplace Politics

One of the hardest lessons I had to learn when I entered the workplace is that some people in a company had personal agendas other than doing their best work. For some, it was to climb the corporate ladder and achieve some high level position. For others, it was to do the least amount of work possible without getting fired. Workplace politics is not easy to understand; just realize that this exists. Try to stay out of it, unless it directly jeopardizes your job or affects your ability to perform your job.

Happy People on the Autism Spectrum have Satisfying Jobs or Hobbies

I N MY TRAVELS TO MANY AUTISM MEETINGS, I HAVE OBSERVED THAT the high-functioning people with autism or Asperger's who make the best adjustments in life are the ones who have satisfying jobs. A job that uses a person's intellectual abilities is great for improving self-esteem. Conversely, the most unhappy people on the spectrum I have met are those who did not develop a good employable skill or a hobby they can share with others. With so much of adult life spent in our jobs, it makes sense that people with satisfying jobs will be happier generally in their life and able to respond better to the different situations that arise.

I have met several successful people on the spectrum who program computers. One Asperger's computer programmer told me she was happy because now she is with "her people." At another meeting, I met a father and son. The father had taught his son computer programming. He started teaching him when he was in the fourth grade and now he works at a computer company. For many people with autism/AS, the way our mind works is well-suited to this profession. Parents and teachers should capitalize on this ability and encourage its development.

Several years ago, I visited autism programs in Japan. I met a large number of high-functioning people on the autism spectrum. Every one of them was employed in a good job. One man translated technical and legal documents. Another person was an occupational therapist and there were several computer programmers. One man who was somewhat less high-functioning works as a baker. What I noticed is that the attitude in Japan is to develop skills. These people with autism/AS benefited from that attitude, and would for the rest of their lives.

While developing an inherent skill into an employable position can be work, it is necessary for people with autism/AS to try hard to do this. However, once they succeed, they must be careful to avoid being promoted from a technical position they can handle well to a management position they cannot handle. I have heard several sad stories of successful people being promoted out of jobs they were good at. These people had jobs such as drafting, lab technicians, sports writing, and computer programming. Once they were required to interact socially as part of their management position, their performance suffered.

Hobbies where people have shared interests are also great in building self-esteem. I read about a woman who was unhappy in a dead-end job. Her life turned around when she discovered that there were other people in the world also interested in her hobby. In her spare time, she breeds fancy chickens. Through the internet, she communicates with other chicken breeders. Even though she still works at her dead-end job, because she explored her hobby, she is now much happier. In my opinion, using the internet for communicating with other hobbyists is much more constructive than griping with other people on the spectrum in a chat room. That doesn't benefit anyone.

Parents and teachers need to place a priority on discovering and then developing the many skills that people with autism or Asperger's possess. These skills can be turned into careers and hobbies that will provide shared interests with other people. This will bring much happiness into the lives of people on the autism spectrum.

Inside or Outside? The Autism/ Asperger's Culture

A FREQUENT TOPIC OF DISCUSSION WITHIN THE AUTISM/ASPERGER'S community is how much people with autism/AS should have to adapt to the world of the "neurotypicals." My view is that you should still be yourself, but there will be changes in behavior that have to be made. Years ago, Dr. Leo Kanner, the person who first described autism, stated that the people who made the best adaptation to the world realized themselves that they had to make some behavioral changes.

This was true for me, too. In 1974, I was hired by a feedlot construction company. My boss made it very clear to me that I had to improve my grooming. I dressed like a slob and paid very little attention to my grooming habits. With the help of some of the secretaries, I learned to dress better and I worked conscientiously to have better personal hygiene. For me, it was a logical process; it followed the **if/then** sequence of a computer code. **If** I wanted my job, **then** I had to change these behaviors. So I did.

Even today, I do not dress the way everybody else does. I like to wear Western clothes; they are my way of expressing myself. Dressing like this is acceptable; being shabby is not. One time I talked to a lady with AS who liked to wear plastic, see-through dresses made in bright Day-Glo colors. Her employer really frowned upon this. She told me that wearing these dresses was part of being who she was. While I understood her desire to retain her individuality, I pointed out to her that her dresses might be okay at a party, but they were inappropriate attire for an office environment. Unless she compromised, her job would be in jeopardy. I suggested a toned-down version of her outfits that would be more socially acceptable at work, such as wearing a conventional dress and decorating it with a few DayGlo accessories, such as a belt, purse or earrings.

Techies versus Suits: the Corporate World

In the corporate world, there is constant friction between technical people, such as computer programmers and engineers, and managers. The tech staff often refer to managers as "suits" (but we don't say this to their faces). Many technical people in large industries have mild autism or Asperger's traits. To them, technical things are interesting and social things are boring. Some of the best times in my life have been spent with other engineers and techies discussing how to build meat plants. The technical people are my social world. We share common personality and behavior traits that provide us with common ground for discussion, and help us better understand each other. (It is also great fun to talk about how most "suits" would be incapable of making a paper bag.)

Every big corporation in a technical field has its department of the social misfits who make the place run. Even a bank has some purely technical people who handle accounting, fix ATMs, and run the computers. There is no black-and-white dividing line between computer nerds or geeks or Asperger's or high-functioning autism. And there will always be friction between the techies and the suits. The suits are the highly social people who rise to the top and become managers. However, they would have nothing to sell and no business to run if they lost all their techies.

Parents, teachers, or others who involve themselves with people with autism/AS need to realize that you cannot turn a non-social animal into a social one. Your focus should be teaching people with autism/AS to adapt to the social world around them, while still retaining the essence of who they are, including their autism/AS. Learning social survival skills is important, but I cannot be something I am not. Social skills teaching methods, such as Carol Gray's Social Stories™, are essential for school-aged kids. These skills should be taught early on. But efforts to enlarge the social world of teens and adults with autism/AS should follow a different path. Rather than focus on their deficiencies, it becomes time to focus on their abilities, and find creative ways to capitalize on their strengths to bring them more into social situations. Some of the bright, socially awkward teenagers need to be removed from the torture chamber of high school and enrolled in technical classes at a community college. This will enable them to be with their true intellectual peers, in fields such as computer programming, electronics, accounting, graphic arts, and other pursuits. Recently, I looked at the catalogue from a community college and all the different, fascinating technical courses would have been great for me in high school.

Some people with autism/AS think in very rigid patterns, and see a particular behavior in an all-or-nothing manner. When we are asked, or expected, to change a behavior, we think that means we need to extinguish it. Most times, that is not the case. It is more that we need to modify the behavior and understand the times and places when it is acceptable, and the times and places when it is not. For instance, I can still dress like a slob in my own home, when no one else is around (a trait I've learned is shared with many neurotypicals). Finding a way to compromise so that we keep our personal nature, but conform to some of the unspoken rules of society (including the workplace), is where our efforts need to be.

People appreciate talent
and being good at something
helps compensate for being weird.

✭

Going to College: Tips for People with Autism & Asperger's

G OING OFF TO COLLEGE CAN BE AN UNNERVING EXPERIENCE FOR people with autism and Asperger's. Usually the high level of help that parents and teachers provide during middle and high school just drops off, and the person can find the transition difficult at best. In this column, I'll share some tips I learned from my college experience.

Teasing

When I was in high school, being teased was torture. Teenagers were hyper-social beings I did not understand. I think that some autistic or Asperger's students who are capable of doing college level work need to be removed from the difficult high school scene. Let them take a few courses at a community college or university. Parents often ask about age restrictions at the college; I learned a long time ago it is better not to ask. Just sign up the student.

Mentors

I had a great science teacher when I was in high school. When the teasing became unbearable, I did science projects in Mr. Carlock's lab. He was often there to help me when I enrolled in college. Having the same mentor in both high school and college was a tremendous help.

Uneven Skills

Many people on the autism continuum have uneven skills. They do well in some subjects and poorly in others. Tutoring may be needed in some subjects. It also may be a good idea to take a lighter course load.

Living at College

My first room assignment in college was with two other roommates. This was a disaster. I could not sleep and I had no peace and quiet. I was then moved to a room with one roommate. This was a much better arrangement. Several of the roommates and I became good friends. A person with autism or Asperger's needs a quiet place to live.

Campus Clubs

I was active in several campus organizations where I was able to use my skills and talents. People appreciate talent and being good at something helps compensate for being weird. When the college put on a musical variety show, I made many of the sets. I also made signs and posters for the ski club and the social committee.

Tips on Classes

I always sat in the front row so I could hear better. It is sometimes difficult for me to hear hard consonant sounds. After class, I always recopied all my notes to help me learn the material. Fluorescent lights did not bother me, but many people with autism or Asperger's cannot tolerate them. The room will appear to flash on and off like a disco, which makes learning during a lecture difficult. Some students have found that placing a lamp next to their chair with an old-fashioned incandescent bulb will help reduce the flicker effect. Wearing a baseball cap with a long visor helps make the fluorescent ceiling lights more tolerable. Tape-record the lecture so it can be listened to later in a room without distractions.

Grooming Skills

You have to learn to not be a slob. Ideally, good hygiene skills should be learned before you go to college. Many grooming activities such as shaving cause sensory discomfort. The person should try different shavers until they find one they can tolerate. It is often more comfortable to use unscented, hypoallergenic deodorant and cosmetics.

Choice of College Major

One problem I have observed is that a person with autism gets through college and then is unable to get a job. It is important to major in a field that will make the person employable. Some good fields are computer science, accounting, library science, and special education. For people going to a community college, take courses such as architectural drafting, computer programming, or commercial art. Get really good at your skill. People respect talent.

Transition from College to Work

The person should start working part-time in their chosen field before they leave college. A slow transition from college to employment will be easier.

The more appropriate
question is "Is my child
ready to drive a car?"

✯

Can My Adolescent Drive a Car?

MANY PARENTS ASK ME ABOUT THE ABILITY OF PEOPLE ON THE autism spectrum to drive a car. I have been driving since I was eighteen. I learned on the dirt roads at my aunt's ranch. Every day for an entire summer, I drove her old pickup truck three miles to the mailbox and back. The truck had a manual gear shift and it would stall unless the clutch was worked just right. Because of the difficult clutch, for the first few weeks my aunt operated the clutch and I sat beside her, learning to steer. After I learned steering, it took me several weeks to master the clutch. Aunt Ann made sure I had completely mastered steering, braking, and changing gears before she let me drive the truck on a paved road with traffic.

The main difference between a typical adolescent and a person with autism is that more time may be required to master the skills involved in driving a car, and these skills may need to be learned one piece at a time. For instance, I didn't drive on a freeway until I was completely comfortable with slower traffic. The several months of driving in the safe, dirt roads on the farm provided the extra time I needed to learn safely.

When a motor skill, such as driving, is being learned, all people have to consciously think about the parts involved, such as steering or operating the clutch. During this phase of motor learning, the brain's frontal cortex is very active. When a skill such as driving or steering becomes fully learned, the person no longer has to think about performing the sequential steps involved. Steering the car becomes automatic and conscious thinking about how to do it is no longer required. At this point, the frontal cortex is no longer activated. The motor cortex takes over when a skill is fully learned and the skill is executed unconsciously.

I would recommend that the process of steering, braking, and otherwise operating a car be fully learned to the "motor automatic" stage before permitting your son or daughter to drive in any amount of traffic, or on a freeway. This helps solve the multitasking requirements involved with driving and frees up the frontal cortex to concentrate on traffic, rather than the operation of the car itself.

If a child can ride a bike safely and reliably obey the traffic rules, he or she can probably drive a car. When I was ten years old, I rode my bike everywhere and always obeyed the rules. Likewise, to be able to drive a car, a person must already know how to steer a bike, golf cart, trike, electric wheelchair, or a toy vehicle. Parents interested in teaching their child to drive a car can plan ahead while the child is still young, making sure he or she first masters some of these skills on other types of vehicles.

Another critical issue to consider is the maturity level of the individual. Does the boy or girl have enough mature judgment to drive a car? Are they careful to obey rules given them? How do they react under pressure? These factors need to be assessed on a case-by-case basis to determine if an adolescent is ready to tackle driving a car. I recommend allowing the person on the spectrum extra time to learn the basic operation of the car and the individual skills involved in driving. After each driving skill becomes fully learned and integrated with the other skills, they can slowly progress to driving on roads with more and more traffic, higher speeds, more frequent stops, or areas where there is a greater chance for different events to occur (for instance, driving in neighborhoods with lots of children or a high concentration of business establishments with cars pulling in and out of parking spaces regularly). Finally, nighttime driving should be avoided until the adolescent is very comfortable with all aspects of daytime driving.

I think rather than pondering *can* my child with ASD drive a car, the more appropriate question is "Is my child *ready* to drive a car?" The act of driving a car can be broken down into small, manageable pieces for instruction. The motor skills can be taught and, with enough practice, can be learned. However, driving is a serious matter, one that involves more than just learned skills. Each parent needs to decide whether or not their son or daughter has the maturity and good judgment required to allow them to get behind the wheel of a car. In this regard, the parents' decision is no different for a person on the spectrum than it would be for a typical child.

Through reading these articles, people with Asperger's also learn that even "normal" people have problems at work that cause stress and must be resolved.

★

Wall Street Journal
Social Stories

M ANY PEOPLE ON THE AUTISM/ASPERGER'S SPECTRUM CAN GET A JOB, but difficulty often arises in keeping it. Everyone working in the field of autism is familiar with Carol Gray's Social Stories™. This method has proved very successful in helping individuals with autism/Asperger's better understand the social world around them. However, there presently exists an urgent need for social stories for autistic adults in the workplace.

The *Wall Street Journal* has been publishing highly relevant and very educational articles to help both employers and employees understand the social dynamics of the workplace. Titles of regular columns have ranged from "Your Career Matters" to "Cubicle Culture." They always contain very good suggestions on how to find and keep a job. They also provide good, functional information on everyday situations that people encounter in the workplace, from dealing with mean bosses to sexual harassment. They have discussed when you should go over your boss's head and the potential consequences. Through reading these articles, people with Asperger's also learn that even "normal" people have problems at work that cause stress and must be resolved. This can alleviate some of the tension experienced within the work setting.

I remember one recent article about gossip and appropriate conversation for the workplace. Conversations that are appropriate at home are not necessarily appropriate at work. Safe topics for casual workplace conversation include sports, the latest movies, computers, and hobbies. Topics that can get you into trouble are sex, other people's health problems, politics, and religion.

The *Journal* contains lots of articles on running a small business and about people who have unique, "niche" businesses. The center column on the front page often focuses on a unique individual. In one issue, a person was featured who had started a business testing pictures from different color printers for fading. He tortured color prints with humidity and different intensities of light and compared results. The businessman described how watching the pattern of colors fading was "exhilarating," and that many print companies were using his services. From reading his comments, it seemed likely to me that he had a mild Asperger's condition.

As more and more individuals are diagnosed along the high-functioning end of the autism/Asperger's continuum, it becomes increasingly important for guidance counselors—especially—to become aware of small business opportunities within their own community. Counselors are often a big influence in guiding students on the spectrum about employment options. Ideal jobs that are less prone to layoffs fall in the fields of auto mechanic, drafting at a local architectural firm, and accounting at a small construction company. As I've mentioned before in my columns, it's crucial that both parents and professionals learn about, and use, the students' interests in particular subjects, and capitalize on their strengths when thinking about future employment options for a teenager or young adult with autism or Asperger's.

I have found reading these *Wall Street Journal* articles to be extremely helpful in increasing my own understanding of workplace dynamics, social/office etiquette, and even more nebulous topics like "office politics." I strongly recommend that counselors and people with high functioning autism or Asperger's subscribe to the *Wall Street Journal* for the valuable information provided within their articles.

Innovative Thinking Paves the Way for AS Career Success

THORKIL SONNE, A FATHER OF A CHILD WITH ASPERGER'S SYNDROME (AS), has founded a business in Denmark called Specialisterne Corporation that employs AS individuals to test new computer programs. Their job is to debug new software and their clients include Cryptomathic, a company that verifies digital signatures, and Case TDC, a major European telephone company. Testing new software is an ideal job for people with AS because the qualities of a good tester are some of the inherent strengths of a person with AS. Aspies have great memories, pay attention to details, are persistent, focused, and love structure.

Thorkil has created an innovative environment that is a win-win solution for both the employees and the corporation's clients. Because all the production employees have some degree of AS, on-the-job stress is reduced dramatically at Specialisterne Corporation. To further avoid daily stress and anxiety, work schedules are planned in advance. All tasks have well-defined goals and they are agreed upon in advance. Specialisterne will hire and train qualified AS job applicants. He uses the Lego Mindstorms programmable robots as a testing tool. That way, job applicants can demonstrate their programming skills with the robots instead of going through a formal interview process.

There are two things that Specialisterne does not tolerate: 1) anger where equipment is damaged or other people are hit, and 2) an individual who constantly stirs up gossip and conflict between coworkers. In return, the Aspies are provided with a work environment where sensory distractions are minimized and they do not have to deal with difficult bosses and complex social situations.

Today Specialisterne has three European offices and it employs twenty people with AS and six neurotypicals to work with the corporate clients.

AS-IT in Lincolnshire, England is another organization working with individuals with AS and high-functioning autism, in this case to train them for information technology positions in large corporations. Because of the "coaching" structure of AS-IT, it helps prevent problems with bosses who do not understand the AS employee. When a corporation hires one of AS-IT's trainees, he or she will still be able to stay in contact with AS-IT for assistance in the job transition as needed. Since the corporation knows they will be getting an AS employee, that, coupled with the increased awareness about autism and AS that AS-IT brings to the corporation, helps prevent misunderstandings when social situations develop that might have previously resulted in an AS individual being fired.

Over the years I have observed that the two main reasons a successful long-term Aspie employee was fired was because of 1) a new, unsympathetic boss and 2) the AS employee was promoted into a job that involved complex social skills and social interaction. The person may have been outstanding in a technical position such as a draftsman or engineer or programmer and he or she failed when promoted into a management position. Employers need to be informed that promotion into management is not the best career path for AS individuals and many technical-type people.

These two corporations are using innovative thinking to design work environments in which people with AS can flourish. The individuals with AS find the support they need in order to be successful and the corporations find brilliant minds that can propel their business forward. Win-win solutions like this are possible when neurotypicals start thinking outside the box and value the positive contributions that AS individuals have to offer.

The way I see it, it is likely that
the genetics that produce autism
are the same genetics that
create an Einstein or a Mozart—
it is more a matter of degree.

The Link Between Autism Genetics and Genius

A S A SOCIETY, WE STILL TEND TO VIEW DISABILITIES IN A NEGATIVE
light. We may use politically correct language and say these people are "challenged" or "differently-abled," but the fact remains that we generally focus more on what they can't do, and tend to overlook the positive traits many of these individuals possess. Such is the case with people with autism and Asperger's Syndrome. If the genetic factors that cause autism were eliminated from the human race, we would pay a terrible price. The way I see it, it is likely that the genetics that produce autism are the same genetics that create an Einstein or a Mozart—it is more a matter of degree. A little of the genetic expression produces highly creative, brilliant thinkers. Too much of the genetics, however, results in severe autism, a nonverbal and much more challenged child.

If Albert Einstein were born today, he would be diagnosed with autism. He had no speech until age three, obsessively repeated certain sentences until the age of seven, and spent hours building houses from playing cards. His social skills remained odd through most of his life, and he was a self-described loner:

"My passionate sense of social justice and social responsibility has always contrasted oddly with my pronounced lack of need for direct contact with other human beings and human communities. I am truly a lone traveler and have never belonged to my country, my home, my friends, or even my immediate family, with my whole heart. ..."

A host of other brilliant historic figures such as Isaac Newton, Thomas Jefferson, Socrates, Lewis Carroll, Glenn Gould, and Andy Warhol are now speculated to have been on the autism spectrum.

Several books have been written that profile famous scientists, musicians, and artists who were on the autism/Asperger's spectrum. In his 2007 release, *Genius Genes: How Asperger Talents Changed the World*, Professor of Psychiatry at Trinity College, Dublin, Michael Fitzgerald, reached the conclusion that ASDs, creativity, and genius were all caused by similar genes, after comparing the characteristics of more than 1,600 people he had diagnosed with known biographical details of famous people. I see it the same way: A mild case of Asperger's Syndrome and being eccentric are the SAME thing, and the positive characteristics of being on the autism spectrum—detailed thinking, unwavering focus, obsessive interests in certain topics—are the very qualities that result in genius thought and world-changing discoveries.

Simon-Baron Cohen, a researcher at the University of Cambridge, England, found that within families of children with autism, there existed a significantly greater number of parents and/or close relatives working as engineers and in other technical professionals. In my family, my grandfather was an MIT-trained engineer who was co-inventor of the automatic pilot for airplanes.

Geeks, nerds, and eccentrics have always been in the world; what has changed is the world itself and our expectations of others within it. I work in a technical field and have worked with many engineers and other technical people who definitely displayed marked characteristics of Asperger's Syndrome. Most of these people are now in their forties, fifties, and sixties—and they are all undiagnosed. They were brought up in an era where social rules were more strictly defined and were carefully taught to all children. This more rigid upbringing actually helped these children acquire enough social skills to get by in the world. Many are successful, and they have held good jobs for years. I know one Asperger's meat plant engineer who keeps a multi-million dollar plant running.

I get worried that today an Asperger's diagnosis may be detrimental to some individuals and hold them back. With greater competition for shrinking numbers of jobs, a person's social capabilities are now looked at as closely as are the person's technical skills or intellectual abilities. The most successful people with mild Asperger's work in places such as Silicon Valley, where superior talent still trumps social skills. Often these individuals have parents who are also in a high-tech field and as the child grew, placed more importance on teaching their children computer programming and other technical skills than worrying about whether or not they had girlfriends or boyfriends or wanted to attend every school dance.

I have given talks at conferences geared to a number of different diagnostic categories such as autism, gifted, and dyslexia. Even though diagnosis is not precise, each diagnostic group lives in its own world. When I go to the book tables, there are very few books stocked on *both* an autism book table and a gifted book table. The books addressing these individuals may be different but I see the same bright Asperger's kids at *both* autism and gifted children meetings. The Asperger's child at the gifted meeting is doing well in school, but the Asperger's child at an autism meeting may be in a poor special ed program, bored, and getting into trouble because adults in his life hold lower expectations of his abilities. Unfortunately, in some cases, people are so hung up on the labels attached to students that they teach to these low expectations and aren't even curious to learn if the child is actually more capable. This is mostly likely to occur when the label is Asperger's instead of gifted but developmentally delayed.

Parents and teachers should look at the child, not the child's label, and remember that the same genes that produce his Asperger's may have given the child the capacity to become one of the truly great minds of his generation. Be realistic with expectations, but don't overlook the potential for genius that may be quietly hiding inside, just waiting for an opportunity to express itself.

✮

REFERENCES

Baron-Cohen, S. 2000. Is Asperger syndrome/high functioning autism necessarily a disability? *Developmental Psychopathology* 12: 480-500.

Einstein, A. 1954. The world as I see it. In *Ideas and opinions, based on mein weltbild.* Carl Seelig, editor. New York: Bonzana Books, pp. 8-11.

Fitzgerald, M., and B. O'Brien. 2007. *Genius genes: How asperger talents changed the world.* Shawnee Mission, KS: Autism Asperger Publishing Company.

Grandin, T. 2006. *Thinking in pictures* (Expanded Edition). New York: Vintage/Random House.

Ledgin, N. 2002. *Aspergers and self-esteem: Insight and hope through famous role models.* Arlington, TX: Future Horizons, Inc. (This book profiles famous scientists and musicians who were probably Asperger's.)

Bibliography

(Unless otherwise noted, all articles appearing in this book are selections from an exclusive column written by Temple Grandin in the award-winning national magazine on ASD, the *Autism Asperger's Digest*. Find information about the Digest at *www.autismdigest.com*.)

Chapter 1. Diagnosis and Early Intervention

Do Not Get Hung up on Labels. In press, September-October 2008 issue

Economical Quality Programs for Young Children with ASD. September-October 2005 issue

Different Types of Thinking in Autism. November-December 2005 issue

Higher Expectations Yield Results. March-April 2007 issue

Chapter 2. Teaching and Education

Autism the Way I See It. November-December 2000 issue

The Importance of Developing Talent. January-February 2001 issue

Teaching People with Autism to be More Flexible. July-August 2002 issue

Teaching Concepts to Children with Autism. November-December 2003 issue

Motivating Students. September-October 2004 issue

Getting Kids Turned On to Reading. November-December 2007 issue

The Importance of Practical Problem-Solving Skills. March-April 2008 issue

Turning Video Game Obsessions into Learning. May-June 2008 issue

Chapter 3. Sensory Issues

Visual Processing Problems in Autism. July-August 2004 issue

Auditory Problems in Autism. November-December 2004 issue

Incorporating Sensory Integration into your Autism Program. March-April 2005 issue

The Effect of Sensory and Perceptual Difficulties on Learning Styles. November-December 2006 issue

Chapter 4. Understanding Nonverbal Autism

You Asked Me! January-February 2002 issue

Tito Lives in a World of Sensory Scrambling. May-June 2005 issue

Solving Behavior Problems in Nonverbal Individuals with Autism. May-June 2005 issue

Whole-Task Teaching for Individuals with Severe Autism. September-October 2007 issue

Chapter 5. Behavior Issues

Disability versus Just Bad Behaviors. May-June 2003 issue

My Experience with Teasing and Bullying. July-August 2001 issue

Rudeness is Inexcusable. May-June 2006 issue

Autism and Religion: Teach Goodness. May-June 2002 issue

Chapter 6. Social Functioning

Insights into Autistic Social Problems. November-December 2002 issue

Learning Social Rules. January-February 2005 issue

Emotional Differences Among Individuals with Autism or Asperger's. September-October 2006 issue

Healthy Self-Esteem. May-June 2007 issue

Four Cornerstones of Social Awareness. July-August 2007 issue

Chapter 7. Medications and Biomedical Therapy

Alternative versus Conventional Medications. March-April 2004 issue
Evaluating Treatments. May-June 2004 issue
Medication Usage: Risk versus Benefit Decisions. July-August 2005 issue

Chapter 8. Cognition and Brain Research

Lose the Social Skills, Gain Savant Skills? September-October 2001 issue
People on the Spectrum Focus on Details. September-October 2002 issue
The Extreme Male Theory of Autism. January-February 2003 issue
Detect Babies at Risk for Developing Autism with Head Measurements. July-August 2003 issue
Thinking in Details. September-October 2003 issue
A Look Inside the Visual-Thinking Brain. January-February 2007 issue

Chapter 9. Adult Issues and Employment

Employment Advice: Tips for Getting and Holding a Job. May-June 2001 issue
Happy People on the Autism Spectrum have Satisfying Jobs or Hobbies. March-April 2002 issue
Inside or Outside? The Autism/Asperger's Culture. November-December 2001 issue
Going to College: Tips for People with Autism & Asperger's. March-April 2001 issue
Can My Adolescent Drive a Car? March-April 2003 issue
Wall Street Journal Social Stories. January-February 2004 issue
Innovative Thinking Paves the Way for AS Career Success. March-April 2006 issue
The Link Between Autism Genetics and Genius. In press, *Autism Asperger's Digest*, July-August 2008 issue

Index

✺ T ✺

✳ W ✳

✳ Y ✳